BREAK THE CYCLE
BEFORE IT BREAKS YOU

UNLOCK THE MINDSET THAT SETS YOU FREE

PRISCILLA MARÍA GUTIÉRREZ, J.D.

CYCLE BREAKER COACH

Some names in my story have been changed for privacy and are notated with an asterisk (*).

TRIGGER WARNING: This book contains details about my traumatic experiences, including substance abuse, sexual assault, eating disorders, and domestic violence. Please practice self-care while reading through its pages and feel free to reach out to me @cyclebreakercoach on social media.

DEDICATION

This labor of love is dedicated to my family:
my parents, Eulalia and Iván J.,
brother, Iván X.,
and fur babies, Nanas and Chules.

CONTENTS

———— ୬୬୯ ————

PART 1

OWN YOUR STORY

ꙮ

Trying to Find My Voice in the Wilderness

Eight days after my nineteenth birthday, I went on a special birthday trip. One beyond my imagination and that I could never forget. At the recommendation of my parents, I agreed to enter a wilderness program to explore my mental health.

I had never been to Utah before, let alone camped outside. The intake process resembles prison in that they ask you to undress, squat, and cough to ensure you do not have any contraband. Contraband in this program includes drugs and weapons but also deodorant, contact lenses, piercings, and razors for shaving.

Yes, using a shared latrine full of everyone's feces and waking up to bloody pants from starting my cycle with no feminine products in sight was hard. But the emotional work was so much harder. New participants are banned from the group and made to observe from afar. They can only join everyone else after they write and share their life stories out loud.

This was the first time I ever sat down and wrote an inventory of my traumas packaged as a rushed memoir. I was the only Latina and, apart from an African-American participant, the only person who wasn't white. This audience of strangers was far from ideal for such a personal share. If the tarantulas and trees could speak, they would have said, "At least let her build trust with the people she's going to pour her fears and tears out to."

But spiders and trees can't talk, and I had no choice anyway. My introduction to the strangers I'd be living outside with wasn't the usual "Hi, my name is Priscilla." It was "I was molested, drank excessively, and feared my brother would die any day." The staff were our wardens in the desert. They decided when we ate, what we ate, what we could talk about, who we could talk to, where we would sleep, and how much we would hike each day.

I knew the staff had the discretion to recommend a longer stay in the desert if I resisted the program rules. So I sat down on the harsh desert floor under some shade and started writing. It's been over a decade, but I remember the words I released onto that black memo pad. This was only one of many invasive and compulsory assignments during my stay. Eventually, the staff tasked me with writing a letter to the deceased pedophile who sexually abused me as a child. In true wilderness therapy fashion, they made me share my letter out loud to the group and they sent a copy to my parents and brother. I had no idea prior to writing the letter that it would be shared with my family. I was mortified to know that they would receive the letter without the opportunity to ask me questions.

Coerced disclosure is an example of *telling your story* but not *owning your story*. I was still unsure if what happened to me was considered molestation when I wrote the letter. I wish I had time to process my molestation before involving my family members. I found other assignments within the program to be more therapeutic than letter writing. For example, a staff member asked me to act like I was drunk so that I could get feedback from group members about my actions.

The other participants had no idea about my assignment. I was curious to see how they would react since I was usually too disconnected from reality when inebriated to assess my behavior in the moment. This exercise, performed in sober clarity and miles away from a drop of liquor, forced me to confront the harmful impact of my "drunken" actions on others. I was the only female group member at this point as members left and joined the group without warning. I managed to, as a staff member put it, have "the guys lined up like a row of ducks" despite being the shortest and physically weakest person present. I realized at this moment that my voice and words can affect people deeply. Although I was pretending to be drunk, the hurt and confusion on my group members' faces were real. I think back to this experience to remind myself to speak with intention and use my voice to help people feel better, not worse.

Overall, the program was more than a lack of hygiene, privacy, and autonomy. This was the first time I confronted my life and received daily feedback on my behavior. I left feeling hopeful that my healing would flow into the roots of our family tree. I wanted my nuclear and extended families to absorb coping strategies and break the silence around their traumas. I will never forget what my father told me before I left the desert. "Don't expect your aunts and uncles to come forward about anything or to support you." Time proved him right.

I completed the program in six weeks and flew back to Maryland. I had nothing to pack up for my trip back home other than confusion, shock, and emotional heaviness. I did not unpack my wilderness experience until recently in therapy. All things considered, I would not recommend the program I participated in to others. I learned far more from Mother Nature than from the staff. It's amazing how everything in the wilderness has an important role within an ecosystem. Trees show us the beauty of letting go, and red ants show us that there is strength in community.

On my flight home I happened to sit directly behind one of my professors and she recognized me. I told her I had just come back from rehab and she was understanding. What are the odds of me running into a professor I had just been in class with a few months earlier at Johns Hopkins? My openness about my healing journey didn't last long. I was terrified for the longest time that someone else at school would learn about my wilderness program experience or that I went to an outpatient rehabilitation program for alcohol afterward.

Years after the wilderness program, when the shock value and intensity of the program wore off, I found myself being similarly closed off and unwilling to accept each detail from my narrative. I was a decade removed from eating dehydrated beans with a dirty stick in Utah before I felt fully comfortable owning my story. My healing journey has been far from a linear path and more like a roller coaster running on faulty electricity. I had to peel back many layers of trauma, confront the most shameful parts of myself, and rediscover myself.

Self-Validation

Introduction to Self-Validation

I was about ten years old when it happened. I was going down the cement staircase outside of our house like I'd done hundreds of times. My maternal grandfather was going down the steps right in front of me. In a blink of an eye, he stumbled over his shoes and went tumbling down until he face-planted onto our asphalt driveway. He didn't move, and I could see a pool of his blood. I remember sitting beside him in the ambulance trying to translate what he was saying in Spanish to English for the paramedic. I was terrified about my grandfather's well-being. He was like a second father to me.

Not too long afterward, I visited the Twin Towers on 9/1/01 with my family, including my grandfather with his healing injuries. I later struggled to understand how the tower I had been at the top of would be completely gone less than two weeks later along with thousands of lives. The stress from my grandfather's near-death fall, helping my mother nurse him back to health, my uncle's passing, and the 9/11 terrorist attacks pushed my little nervous system beyond its limits. My body didn't have the energy to suppress memories I didn't even know were suppressed.

Eventually, I found the courage to confide in one of my elders about my grandfather "touching me" previously in Ecuador and California. They listened, asked questions, and the next morning said, "That wasn't molestation." That is where the conversation ended and where my self-distrust started. For years, I replayed what happened to me and felt so confused. *Why do I feel like this if it wasn't molestation? If it wasn't molestation, what was it?* I *finally* received clarity when I was forced to send the letter about my grandfather's abuse to my parents and brother at the wilderness program.

Years later, the elder I confided in described the cult of silence that they grew up in. They had kept their own sexual trauma hidden for decades. By not holding my grandfather accountable, this elder silenced me and perpetuated a generational cycle of protecting abusers in the family. The fog of confusion around my grandfather's abuse dimmed my inner light. I lost the ability to speak and trust my truth.

I sought validation from others—family, friends, therapists—for most of my life. Consider these reactions I received from people who knew about my molestation. An aunt told me, "My father was not a bad guy. He wasn't a killer." An uncle said, "You've never been through anything. You've always had it easy." A friend concluded, "I think what you went through was worse than my rape because your grandfather did it to you."

Depending on who you asked, my molestation was either the worst thing imaginable or it hadn't stopped me from having an easygoing life. These mixed responses illustrate the hazards of seeking external

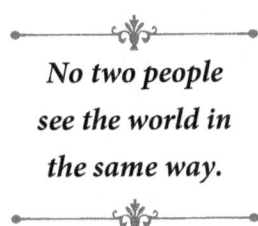

No two people see the world in the same way.

validation. No two people see the world in the same way. News stations describe the same event in vastly different ways based on their target audience and brand. Similarly, others view the world through a lens of unique experiences, biases, and values.

My aunt experienced sexual abuse by my grandfather. Instead of "I'm sorry we didn't protect you from him. I wasn't protected from him either," she offered words that helped her love the only father she knew. My uncle experienced a traumatic upbringing in Nicaragua. He protected my grandmother from machete attacks, dodged bullets from AK-47s, and experienced homelessness due to the *Revolución Nicaragüense* (Nicaraguan Revolution). In his eyes, the woes of a suburban girl pale in comparison to a fatherless refugee who had to survive in Los Angeles. My friend suffered date rape. She understood the pain, anger, and overwhelm that comes with surviving sexual assault. I was shocked when she described my molestation as worse than her rape. She held space for me in a way I hadn't experienced before and acknowledged the extra layer of pain that comes with incest.

Self-validation has been a game-changer for my healing. The practice involves *accepting your feelings, thoughts, and perceptions as legitimate without needing anyone else to co-sign.* It's a revolutionary step for those of us who grew up in an emotionally invalidating environment where emotional abuse like gaslighting was rampant. Self-validation is a radical act of self-love. It is you asserting yourself as the most credible authority over your experiences. To self-validate is to recognize and tell the world, "I am the expert on my mind, body, and experiences. I am the most qualified to describe what happened to me and how I felt about it."

I now know that the only person's description of my molestation that matters is Little Priscilla. She was there. It was her body. She remembers. And, according to her, the molestation she endured was every part devastating and violent. I have learned to be selective of who I trust with my experiences because not everyone is capable of holding a safe space for trauma survivors, including some mental health practitioners.

Unfortunately, I've experienced invalidation during some of my most vulnerable moments: inside a therapist's office. The following are examples of invalidating comments I've received over the years from therapists:

> ➢ **Blame for Sexual Assault:** Some therapists assigned partial blame to me for being sexually assaulted. Yes, people that were not present in the city, let alone inside the room, where I was sexually assaulted were telling *me* what happened to *my* body. Their comments include, "I mean look at you, you

were torturing the guy being next to him in bed." While another refused to acknowledge a sexual trauma I disclosed as sexual assault because I "rely too much on labels" and "why can't it be enough to just say the experience sucked?"

> **Bisexual Erasure:** I discussed my sexuality with multiple therapists. The confusion I experienced around my molestation extended to my sexuality. I knew how I felt about my experiences with women, but I struggled to validate these feelings. During a therapeutic conversation, my therapist said, "You are not bisexual. You don't talk like you're bisexual." I accepted her determination as my truth just as I had with my family member's misjudgment of my sexual trauma. I fell into a hole of secrecy and insecurity in both situations.

> **Assertion of Their Opinion as Fact:** Several therapists overstepped their role by dictating my intentions and feelings during therapy sessions. For example, Dr. Outofpocket* dismissively told me, "You don't remember him because you didn't want to remember him" in response to a sexual trauma I experienced as a freshman in college. In reality, I don't remember this guy clearly because 1) I was drunk, and 2) the brain's fear response can alter memory encoding during a traumatic event. It's common for a trauma survivor to have fragmented or incomplete memories of the event.[1] My hazy memory was not a choice but a defense mechanism.

---

[1] "Neurobiology of Trauma," University of Northern Colorado, https://www.unco.edu/assault-survivors-advocacy-program/learn_more/neurobiology_of_trauma.aspx.

Seeking external validation is a gamble. You could leave the conversation feeling accepted and understood if their response included the words you had longed to hear. On the other hand, you could leave the conversation feeling judged and defeated if they echo your inner critic and invalidate, judge, or minimize your experience.

Self-validation is like a muscle. This muscle grows stronger each time you lean into confidence and self-belief. Some of us have an atrophied or nonexistent self-validation muscle as a consequence of surviving or witnessing unhealthy relationships. Regardless of your starting point, start hitting those reps. Reps could include honoring your nervous system, valuing your voice, compassionate self-talk, and setting boundaries. For example, you could say, "I want to share about a painful experience I had. I just need someone to listen and don't need any advice or feedback." Setting boundaries is essential because your emotional safety and wellness could be at risk.

Self-validation could be a catalyst for your healing and bridge the gap between who you are and who you are becoming. What better repellant to unnecessary suffering is there than self-validation? Think about it. How many times were your actions driven by insecurities? How often do you let someone else's words influence whether you have a good or bad day? How much of your self-image has been painted by someone else? Growing up I experienced bullying and microaggressions. Little Priscilla believed what others told her.

She believed her peers who called her a "bitch," "wetback," and "ugly." She didn't question her friend's father who said he didn't want his daughter to hang out with me because I was "Black." She didn't push back when her sixth-grade best friend's mother ensured we wouldn't have any classes together because of my alleged bad influence. Droplets of disrespect collected inside Little Priscilla's emotional cup until it overflowed like a raging river when she entered womanhood.

Adult Priscilla understands that someone's verbal daggers are a projection of the speaker's internal world. Eleanor Roosevelt once said, "No one can make you feel inferior without your consent." To add to what Roosevelt said, you are the gatekeeper of your peace and wellness. Self-validation is an opportunity to gift ourselves the words, actions, and closure we seek from others. It is key to our healing, growth, and emotional freedom. Self-validation is not about dismissing others' feedback or discrediting perspectives that don't align with yours. Self-validation is about anchoring yourself in self-confidence, self-trust, and self-advocacy regarding your experiences and feelings. It is a transferable skill that can enhance our personal and professional lives.

Self-Validation Is a Superpower

I devalued my opinions, perspectives, and experiences for the majority of my life. I doubted my discernment ever since my molestation was not taken seriously. As the years passed and my grandfather died, I realized that the elder I had initially confided in about my molestation made an inaccurate conclusion. What happened to Little Priscilla was categorically, objectively, and criminally molestation. The invalidation around my molestation ignited a guilt complex that persisted into my adulthood.

Consequently, I often blamed myself when things went wrong or when wrong was done to me.

For instance, when I was an adult, I was raped—and I denied it for years. I echoed the invalidation I received from therapists and blamed myself. It was too painful to accept that I'd been violated in the worst way by the man I'd given my all to, had shared my deepest traumas with, had welcomed into my family, and had planned marriage with. I invested far too many hours, tears, and miles

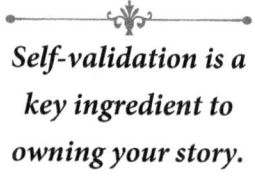

Self-validation is a key ingredient to owning your story.

desperately trying to change my reality. Nothing could change the fact that I had been raped by my boyfriend. The only fact I could change was my acceptance. I was in that dark apartment room alone with him. It happened to me.

Validating my rape was a turning point. It marked a shift from submitting to the opinions of others to affirming and asserting my truth. I wasn't going to let any more therapists or family members dictate my experiences, feelings, or thoughts.

Self-validation is a key ingredient to owning your story. It's the difference between boldly writing your autobiography and someone writing your unofficial biography.

I spent years governed by pain. Unhealed trauma stole my sense of safety, diminished my confidence, and warped my self-image. Consequently, I found myself not attracting but *accepting* toxic dynamics in my personal and professional relationships. I overlooked how my nervous system responded to certain people to maintain the status quo. I viewed my flaws as irreparable instead of growth opportunities. I focused on repairing others' flaws and encouraging their growth. My relationships were ultimately a reflection of how I viewed and treated myself.

No, you are not "crazy." Trauma rewired your brain.

DIMINISHED PREFRONTAL CORTEX:
- Trouble regulating fear and other emotions

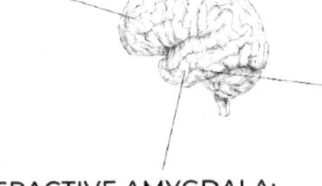

REDUCED HIPPOCAMPUS:
- Difficulty differentiating between trauma flashbacks and present reality

OVERACTIVE AMYGDALA:
- Rational thinking compromised by hypervigilance and other intense stress responses

I did my best with what I knew and what I had at the time. Dr. Maya Angelou said, "Do the best you can until you know better. Then when you know better, do better." I didn't start to know or do better until I started therapy. Dialectical Behavior Therapy (DBT) was especially helpful in my healing process. I became equipped with tools to curb self-destructive behaviors and thoughts. DBT is a structured and evidence-based treatment that focuses on skills for distress tolerance, emotional regulation, interpersonal effectiveness, and mindfulness.

For instance, "radical acceptance" is a DBT skill that requires participants to wholly accept circumstances outside of their control without judgment, even if those circumstances are painful or uncomfortable.

Regardless if you believe in God, it is a fact that you are not God. No one person can control everything. Radical acceptance helped me to identify what is within my control. I cannot control how people treat me, view me, or speak about me. I can, however, control how I treat myself, view myself, and speak to myself. I realized that self-validation is a shield of armor that protects against self-doubt and self-sabotage. For example, it's valid to recognize and process trauma weeks, months, or even years after you experienced the traumatic event.

Self-acceptance is not a destination you can point to on a map. It is a journey that will meander, ebb, and flow. Be patient with yourself as your brain rewires, unlearns, and rebuilds. Some days will be harder than others to love who you see in the mirror. Perfection is

Be patient with yourself as your brain rewires, unlearns, and rebuilds.

not the goal. Cumulative progress, growth, and transformation are the inspiration. It matters less that you slip or fall along the way. What matters is that you continue the momentum forward and do not give up on yourself.

Developing Self-Validation Skills

Self-validation is a skill set that requires consistency, repetition, and strategy. Below are ways to develop your self-validation skills:

➢ **Positive Self-Talk:** How you speak to yourself is vital. Your internal dialogue could motivate you to climb Mount Everest or lure you into the deepest depths of depression. My internal dialogue echoed the external invalidation I received over the years. Eventually, I started to turn the dial down on my inner critic and amplify my inner coach. This sounded like "I hold the wisdom I need" instead of "I should ask someone if I'm being dramatic." This mental shift could understandably feel awkward or insincere at first. It will take time to master a new language so different from the one you've been speaking for years. Be patient and consistent. The self-empowerment is worth it.

➢ **Journaling:** They say some things are better left unsaid. In that case, write them down. Sometimes pen and paper provide the refuge someone needs to make it through another day. You can give yourself a judgment-free zone within the bounds of a journal. Remember this is not a submission for the *New York Times*. Your grammar and spelling do not matter. What matters is releasing your feelings and attaching words to your

> *Sometimes pen and paper provide the refuge someone needs to make it through another day.*

thoughts. Journaling is an effective way to empty your emotional bucket and reduce overwhelm. A quick Google search can yield countless journal prompts on almost any topic you can think of. Whether it's an aesthetically pleasing planner or a napkin, allow the thoughts to flow into consonants and vowels.

➤ **Mindfulness Practices:** Have you ever played with a Chinese finger trap before? It's a small tube made from woven bamboo where you put your index fingers on either end. The tube closes in when you attempt to pull your fingers out. But the tube loosens up if you push your fingers toward each other. For many of us, the left index finger represents the past, the right index finger represents the future, and the tube represents our mind. In other words, many of us are constantly torn between rumination and future-tripping, which robs us of the present. Mindfulness strategies help us to lean into the moment and, like the finger trap, become less tense. Some mindfulness techniques to add to your wellness toolbox include deep breathing, meditation, Emotional Freedom Technique (EFT) tapping, and yoga.

Cultivating self-awareness is key to self-validation because you need to understand what you are trying to accept and acknowledge about yourself. Self-awareness requires being in tune with your nervous system, mindset, and decision-making. Achieving this internal harmony is especially challenging for trauma survivors who may have nervous system dysregulation. Start by being curious about yourself, asking self-reflective questions and taking note of who you are. For example, what topics activate your nervous system, what patterns do you notice in your relationships, or what habits are interfering with your goals?

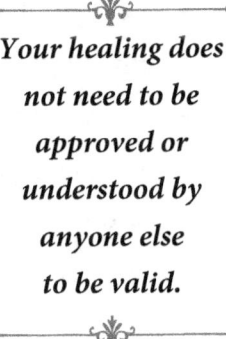

Your healing does not need to be approved or understood by anyone else to be valid.

As you continue reading, remember that no two people on earth are walking the same path. Your journey to self-acceptance and healing may look nothing like your best friend's or your mother's. Consider your experience like a thumbprint, unique and fully yours. There is no shortage of opinions in this world.

Your healing journey will not be immune to assumptions or judgments. The good news is that your healing does not need to be approved or understood by anyone else to be valid.

One tactic I use to foster self-acceptance is to talk to myself the way I would to a close friend or my inner child.

Practice Self-Compassion

Someone once said, "If I asked you to name all the things you love, how long would it take you to name yourself?" Years ago, I would have not even thought to include my name. Nowadays, I make it a point to put myself first. How did I go from harming to admiring myself? Self-compassion.

➤ Trauma healing is more than just resolving painful memories.

➤ It's recovering from the addictions you relied on to cope.

➤ It's managing the chronic illnesses you developed from stress.

➤ It's reconnecting with the parts of yourself you abandoned to survive.

➤ Trauma recovery is about developing a compassionate inner voice that gifts you what self-loathing robbed you of—emotional safety, healing, and genuine connection.

I was compassion-deficient for many years despite practicing forgiveness of others and volunteering. I denied myself the grace and kindness I readily gave to others. Being stingy with self-compassion is not a sustainable way to live. Eventually, your body, mind, and spirit will feel the burden of self-shame. We have options in the face of self-loathing and pain. We can choose to wrap ourselves in the warmth of encouraging words, a growth mindset, self-care, or all of the above. Self-compassion is not about dodging accountability or luxurious self-indulgence. It's about extending to yourself the understanding and softness you would offer a friend.

I would never blame anyone for their sexual assault, starve them, or encourage them to stay in a toxic relationship. Yet I made myself an exception to the grace I freely gave others. My body heard and felt every brutal syllable I said to myself. Harsh self-talk reverberated throughout my nervous system and eroded my self-confidence. Eventually, I realized that the way I speak to myself matters and I would remain unhappy until I swapped self-loathing and judgment with self-compassion and understanding. I am

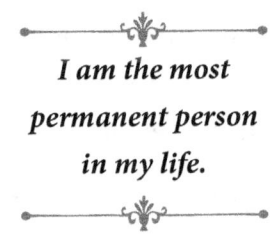

I am the most permanent person in my life.

the most permanent person in my life. It serves my joy to live in a body that feels safe and appreciated.

My inner voice as a twenty-year-old was so overcritical and rigid that it didn't even occur to me that my sexual trauma as an adult was not my fault. I blamed myself for drinking and being in areas I shouldn't have been in. I had internalized the victim-blaming that echoed on social media and from peers. This solitary echo chamber didn't allow me to connect with myself or others on a deeper level. Negative self-talk kept me hurt and detached. Can you relate? Does your chest tighten, jaw clench, or heart rate increase when you speak unkindly to yourself? Updating the software your mindset runs on is crucial.

Take a moment to assess your internal dialogue. According to Dr. Kristin Neff and Dr. Christopher Germer, founders of the Center for Mindful Self-Compassion, self-compassion refers to a kind and

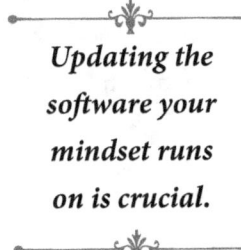

Updating the software your mindset runs on is crucial.

understanding attitude toward oneself during times of pain or failure. In a 2017 study, they found that higher levels of self-compassion among individuals were linked to lower levels of mental health issues, such as depression, anxiety, and stress. Additionally, a strong correlation existed between the practice of self-compassion and the likelihood of engaging in personal development activities.[2]

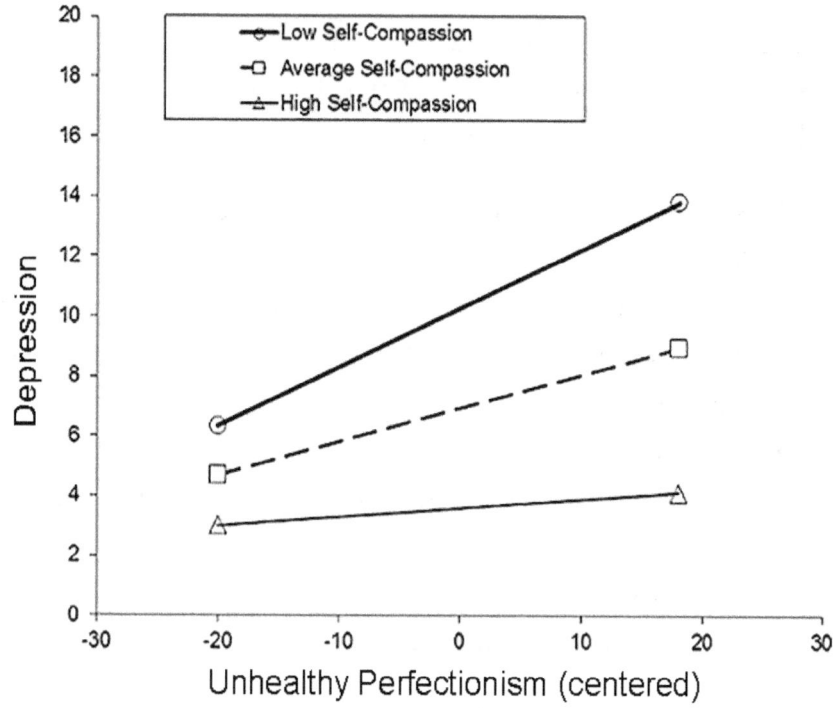

FIGURE 1: THE EFFECT OF SELF-COMPASSION ON
PERFECTIONISM AND DEPRESSION[3]

The researchers concluded that self-compassion coupled with personal growth could lead to more sustainable mental health

---

[2] Kristen D. Neff and Christopher Germer, "Self-Compassion and Psychological Wellbeing," in James R. Doty (Ed.) *Oxford Handbook of Compassion Science* (Oxford University Press, 2017), chapter 27.

[3] Madeleine Ferrari et al., "Self-compassion moderates the perfectionism and depression link in both adolescence and adulthood," *PloS One* 13, no. 2 (2018): e0192022.

benefits than efforts solely aimed at "fixing" oneself or others. These findings demonstrate how self-compassion engenders mental wellness and promotes continuous personal development. Adopting a loving inner voice is a journey in itself that involves unlearning and disinheriting thoughts that have been playing on a loop for years or even generations. It's far easier said than done but it is possible. Fundamentally, self-compassion is about being open to other perspective and possibilities about yourself. For instance, I mistook trauma responses like angry outbursts and selective mutism as my personality for years. Understanding and validating my trauma opened up doors to self-forgiveness.

A psychiatrist diagnosed me with Obsessive Compulsive Disorder (OCD) when I was twenty-seven years old. My OCD episodes included hours spent compulsively "checking" my intrusive thoughts, debilitating anxiety, paranoia, and loss of appetite. Living with OCD felt akin to an addiction. OCD hijacked my rational thinking, strangled me with stubborn delusions, and robbed me of clarity, peace, and self-trust. Eventually, I cracked under the weight of irrational, incessant thoughts and confided in my parents. This vulnerable act was a leap toward breaking the silence that fed my shame.

The seeds that culminated in a panicked twenty-eight-year-old with OCD sobbing on the floor of a public bathroom were planted long ago—memories of my pedophile grandfather falling and almost dying as I watched helplessly, followed by a traumatic ambulance ride and months of helping my mother nurse him back to health. Little Priscilla experienced intrusive thoughts, panic, crying spells, and developed a phobia of blood that persists today.

Little Priscilla eventually told a family member about how she would tap and count repetitively. They thought it was weird and also asked another family member *"¿Por qué sigue llorando la Priscilla?"* ("Why does Priscilla keep crying?") I was too young to advocate for myself then. Adult Priscilla understands that Little Priscilla was self-soothing in the aftermath of her traumas and experiencing PTSD symptoms. I needed professional mental health support. Ultimately, I learned to suppress my traumas, lean on others to validate my experiences, and take care of those who have hurt me. These unhealthy behavior patterns followed me into adulthood.

Living and existing are two different states. I existed for the majority of my life as a wallflower—observing but rarely connected to my surroundings. I did not honor my hunger, stress, or fatigue cues on countless occasions. I'd often go into a freeze response when I felt overwhelmed which meant not speaking and staying still.

Statistically, I have crossed paths with umpteen trauma survivors. But connecting to yourself is a prerequisite to connecting with others. I missed out on opportunities to feel less alone with other trauma survivors by distracting myself with destructive behaviors and relationships. True healing and connection happen once we acknowledge and accept our inner experiences with kindness and empathy.

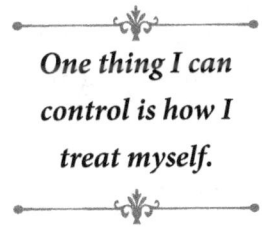

One thing I can control is how I treat myself.

The amount of things I cannot control outnumber the stars in the sky. But one thing I can control is how I treat myself. Self-care elevated me from existing to living and from an empty shell of myself to a woman full of compassion and hope. Self-affirmations, journaling, support groups, and movement are ways I let my body know it can count on me. Self-compassion and a growth mindset can turn a tragedy into an opportunity and shame into wisdom.

Self-Love Is a Verb

"Opposite action" is my favorite DBT skill. It helps someone cope with a difficult situation by doing the opposite of what their emotional or biological response is telling them to do. For instance, an angry person might prepare themselves to physically attack someone. Opposite action in this situation could look like leaning into calmness and kindness through deep breathing. There have been many times when I chose to socialize with loved ones despite a strong urge to isolate myself or pursued a goal that my fears told me to give up.

Opposite action illustrates that self-love is a verb. It's possible to act kindly to yourself even when your mind is flooded with self-sabotaging thoughts. One technique I use to practice opposite action is to dedicate my actions to my inner child, Little Priscilla. Little Priscilla reminds me of how lovely it feels to be present, curious, playful, and happy. It's easy for me to be harsh and critical of Big Priscilla. But I would never want to hurt, neglect, or punish Little Priscilla. She deserves to eat nutritious meals, surround herself with love, be in nature, and feel safe.

Knowing your self-love language is helpful in practicing opposite action. Dr. Gary Chapman coined the five love languages:

1. words of affirmation
2. physical touch
3. gifts
4. acts of service
5. quality time

For example, physical touch as an act of self-love could include wrapping yourself up in a soft blanket or practicing a skincare routine, whereas quality time could include going on a solo walk or reading a book. Mindfulness is another way to deepen your self-love. Mindfulness refers to being aware of your thoughts and feelings in the moment without judgment. Breath work is an effective mindfulness practice because we can only take a breath in the present. We cannot retake a past breath or take a breath thirty years from now. Self-love means appreciating yourself for taking action, no matter how big or small, instead of putting yourself down for not meeting or exceeding your expectations.

> *Self-love means appreciating yourself for taking action, no matter how big or small, instead of putting yourself down for not meeting or exceeding your expectations.*

Author James Clear said, "It's better to do less than you hoped than nothing at all."[4] As a recovering perfectionist, I have spent too much time hurling harsh criticism at myself. For example, I could not enjoy my workouts when I was active in my eating disorder. I would fixate on the number of calories I burned, how many minutes I spent on a machine, and what I ate. I felt like I was walking a tightrope during each workout because my body internalized any slight deviation from my workout and calorie regimen as a massive failure. Nowadays, I exercise to feel good, relieve stress, and build strength. I do not fixate on metrics or put myself down if I don't exercise for a few days.

How did I make a 180-change on my self-love journey? For starters, it was less like turning a dial and more like dropping the dial on the floor, picking it up, losing it in the ocean, recuperating it, and then finding out the dial unlocks a room full of exactly what you needed all along. Ebbs, flows, peaks, and valleys are par for the course of a self-love journey. It's a long, winding road with no clear destination but is worth the lifelong effort because the relationship you have with yourself is the longest one you will ever have.

I made the goalpost for my self-love adventure as progress and balance and kept motivated by setting short-term goals. Something I have wanted to do for a long time was bungee jumping. I finally took the literal leap and signed up by myself in 2023. I hiked ten miles to jump off the Bridge to Nowhere outside

---

[4] James Clear, *Atomic Habits: An Easy and Proven Way to Build Good Habits and Break Bad Ones* (Penguin, 2018), 165.

of Los Angeles. This hike included crossing what felt like freezing water, crawling on all fours, and weathering the heat. Needless to say, we had to take multiple breaks to replenish our energy. I was able to complete this arduous hike by setting shorter targets. Focusing on making it to the top of a hill, the other side of a creek, or beyond a specific boulder is far less intimidating than accepting I had to complete 20,000 steps to slip a harness on, throw myself off a bridge, and hope for the best.

My Bridge to Nowhere experience parallels my self-love journey in many ways. Although a self-love journey focuses on you, it's not meant to be a solo trip. Multiple people lent me a hand during the hike. My venture would not have been possible had I tried to do everything by myself. Similarly, we need our chosen family to lean on as we nurture self-love. I've also reached for the generational gifts hanging from my family tree whenever my motivation dulls or self-doubt takes over. My ancestral roots grew from sunshine and rainstorms. I tap into the resilience and creativity encoded in my DNA whenever I feel tempted by self-sabotage. I think of my grandmothers and the radical acts of self-love they did.

We need our chosen family to lean on as we nurture self-love.

My paternal grandmother, Gloria Esperanza Solorzano, made the life-changing and lifesaving decision to flee alongside her three sons and mother from a wartorn Nicaragua in December of 1979. She left behind her possessions and the only home she knew for the sake of her sons who would be inevitably drafted into the *Revolución Nicaragüense*. My grandmother grew up with a silver spoon in Nicaragua but cleaned hotels and worked in oppressive factories in Los Angeles to make ends meet. Mita, as we called her, made the impossible happen without the help of my abusive and unfaithful grandfather. She did not let public opinion discourage her from starting over in another country or getting a divorce.

My maternal grandmother, Bertha María Peñafiel, survived domestic violence, the loss of two children, and other unspoken traumas growing up in Ecuador. She made the challenging decision to relocate my mother and aunt from Riobamba, Ecuador, to Los Angeles for a better life. Legally, my grandmother committed parental kidnapping because she took my mother and aunt without telling anyone, including my mother, aunt, and grandfather. My grandfather had a history of committing sexual assault toward female family members and physical assault toward my grandmother.

Both my grandmothers were refugees in different ways and fled to California in hopes of providing their children with safety and opportunity without the support of their once husbands. Divorcing and sidestepping the "man of the household" was socially unacceptable in their Catholic, Latin-American communities. My grandmothers remind me that nobody can shame a woman who is unashamed of her identities, experiences, or actions. They help me remember that I have the inner resources to achieve the dreams that make me nervous to speak out loud.

Recovery Is Self-Discovery

I was under the influence of pain way before I first drank alcohol. My binge drinking was a symptom of unhealed wounds. The true gateway drug was my unresolved trauma. Binge drinking was a subconscious way of keeping me in the freeze trauma response state I experienced during my molestation. Sometimes I wonder if shame kills more people than addiction. I realized trauma was the fuel for my self-destruction when I subconsciously replaced alcohol use disorder with an eating disorder.

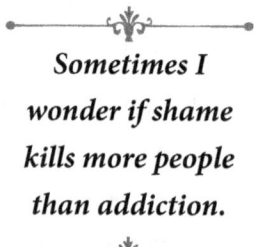

Sometimes I wonder if shame kills more people than addiction.

Unhealthful coping mechanisms are like icebergs. A "self-destruction" iceberg's exposed tip is where we observe drinking and other numbing activities—gambling, high-risk sex, compulsive shopping, and self-harm. Beneath the surface and behind the mask is the root of that self-sabotage, such as untreated mental illness and unresolved trauma. The source of self-sabotage does not melt away over time without intervention. Instead, the chaos compounds.

Trauma recovery does not happen through silence, stigma, or repression. Healing requires authenticity, self-care, support, and an internal revolution. I lived most of my life lacking emotional regulation skills. I did not have a solid understanding of self-care, conflict resolution, or stress management. Neither did my parents and neither did my parents' parents. Younger versions of myself did not know self-validation was an option.

I relied on authority figures like elders, teachers, and therapists to approve my feelings and confirm if an experience was traumatic or if I reacted justifiably. Ultimately, placing someone else in the driver's seat of my experiences left me vulnerable to manipulation and compromised self-trust.

That is not to say that others' perspectives and observations are worthless when healing. Being receptive to the feedback of trustworthy people has been helpful in my recovery journey. My mother has played a crucial role in my healing by providing honest observations and input about my life. Keeping an open mind to her feedback has helped me recognize patterns of behavior that I would have not otherwise realized.

Self-healing is a lifelong adventure with no finish line to cross. Life by design is unpredictable. You might find another challenge on your path after surmounting an obstacle. Life will not get any more predictable once you go to therapy or practice yoga. Tragedies and blessings will continue to happen. As the Greek philosopher Heraclitus said, "The only constant in life is change." Embracing shifts, developments, and unexpected turns instead of resisting sets you up for growth, resilience, and transformation. The change happens inside you.

You have the potential to become more resilient and better surf what life throws at you. Life doesn't get easier; instead, you get stronger. Imagine how much wisdom you can earn when you walk around with an open mind and spirit. Imagine who you can become. No one can experience healing for you. No one can revolutionize your mindset for you. You are in the pilot's seat to navigate how you nurture your mind, body, and spirit.

Aim to expand your emotional toolbox, build self-trust, find non-destructive sources of dopamine, and cultivate reciprocal relationships that help you navigate life's plot twists. Build trust with yourself and your inner child by following through with your word. Show yourself what you are capable of and how resilient you are. Revisiting the past is part of healing, but remember there are plenty of wonderful days ahead of you. You have

Revisiting the past is part of healing, but remember there are plenty of wonderful days ahead of you. You have not seen what tomorrow has in store yet.

not seen what tomorrow has in store yet. Let the universe show you how good it can get.

Summary and Self-Care

Recap:

> *"There is no greater agony than bearing an untold story inside you."*
>
> ~ Dr. Maya Angelou

Embrace Self-Compassion and Acceptance

➢ Include yourself in the compassion you put out into the world.

➤ Reframe imperfections as opportunities for growth and reminders of your humanity.

➤ Identify and challenge negative self-talk. Lean into the belief that these negative thoughts are not facts.

➤ Embrace self-acceptance as a necessary step in self-empowerment and liberation.

Prioritize and Advocate for Your Mental Wellness

➤ Value mental and physical health equally. They are interdependent and key to your overall well-being.

➤ Seek professional support for your mental health needs.

➤ Contribute positively to mental health conversations and initiatives to break the silence and stigma persistent in many communities.

➤ Set a healthy precedent for personal and professional relationships by strengthening the relationship you have with yourself.

Cultivate Personal Growth and Resilience

➤ Prioritize continuous learning, personal development, and community connection.

➤ Reframe obstacles and setbacks as opportunities for growth and learning.

➤ Gain resilience and wisdom from negative and positive experiences.

➤ Celebrate your achievements, milestones, and every time you get back up.

Create Genuine Connections

➢ Set and maintain firm boundaries in personal and professional relationships.

➢ Communicate assertively and authentically with others.

➢ Nurture a supportive network through community engagement and reciprocity.

➢ Be generous with your wisdom and support.

Cycle Breaker Challenge: Set Your S.M.A.R.T. Goals

Goals are your North Star steadily guiding and motivating you on an unpredictable path.

An effective way to set and structure goals is through the S.M.A.R.T. goals framework created by George T. Doran, which stands for Specific, Measurable, Achievable, Relevant, and Time-bound goals.

Here is a self-care challenge to help you fine-tune your goal-setting abilities:

➢ **Specify Three Self-Validation Goals:** Brainstorm which aspects of your self-relationship need more tender loving care. Perhaps you want to build self-trust, set firmer boundaries, or explore your gifts. Pick your three guiding stars.

➢ **Transform Each Goal into a S.M.A.R.T. Goal**

    ○ **Specific:** Specify exactly what aspect of self-validation the goal addresses and what actions you will take to accomplish the goal. For instance, "I will counter a self-deprecating comment with three self-appreciating compliments to build my self-trust."

o **Measurable:** Decide how you will measure data to track your progress. Some common ways to quantify your growth include visual trackers like crossing off days on a calendar, journaling, and using a goal-tracking app. For example, you could memorialize an instance where you trusted yourself in a journal entry.

o **Achievable:** Set targets that you can reach. I would not set a goal to become an Olympic track runner because I know I do not have the skills or resources to become one. Similarly, establish self-validation goals that you can realistically complete within a specific time frame. For instance, you could practice yoga twice a week for two months to improve self-awareness of your internal experience.

o **Relevant:** Choose goals that align with your broader life plans and aspirations. Each goal should be meaningful, motivating, and pertinent to where you are in life. For example, you might feel motivated to improve your mindfulness if you are in a relationship and want to connect more deeply with your partner.

o **Time-bound:** Designate a time frame to accomplish each goal that creates a sense of urgency and purpose. Setting milestones along the way could also help you maintain momentum. For instance, "I want to set firm boundaries with four family members around my personal life in the next eight weeks. I'd like to set boundaries with two family members by the four-week mark."

➢ **Write Your Goals Down:** Document your goals intentionally such as writing them on sticky notes across your home, listing them on a whiteboard in your bedroom, or setting a picture of your vision board as your cellphone wallpaper. These reminders could help you stay focused against distractions, overcome resistance, and gain clarity.

➢ **Share Your Goals with Others:** Tell at least one supportive person your goals, especially someone you look up to. Goal-sharing could provide several benefits such as accountability, motivation, feedback, and guidance. I am a coach who has a coach. I am writing this book on a Friday night right now because I set a goal with my coach to write two pages daily. I also agreed to pay a fine if I did not reach my goal for further incentivization.

➢ **Reflect and Adjust Accordingly:** Most people focus on setting and accomplishing goals but neglect to evaluate and adjust their goals along the way. It's okay to modify your goals if circumstances change or your values shift.

PART 2
BE YOUR FIERCEST ADVOCATE

———— ꙮ ————

My Brother's Near-Death Experience

I received a shocking call on January 14, 2012. The call was shocking in the sense that it overwhelmed my nervous system but not in that it was unexpected. I anticipated this call for years. My body remembers the day as if it happened within the last forty-eight hours. I was alone in my dorm listening to Aretha Franklin and studying for the LSAT, the entrance exam for law school, when my phone rang.

"Priscilla, I'm calling you to tell you that Iván was found unresponsive. We don't know what's going on, but we think he's in a coma." I didn't know what to do. I stood in front of the sink unsure if I needed to throw up. I didn't have time to think about how I felt. I was car-less and needed to get to the DC suburb he was being treated at immediately. I remember everything.

The blood transfusions.

The fecal catheter.

The ventilator and the IV lines.

The doctor's words that mercilessly cut through my body.

"He has a zero chance of recovery."

"You are prolonging your agony by not taking him off life support."

"This is the worst MRI I've seen in my career."

I came to resent the word "reflex."

I would get excited when I saw him smile or move around like he was about to wake up from a deep dream. Doctors would quickly say, "No, that's just a reflex. It doesn't mean anything." I spoke to my brother for six months not knowing if he'd ever respond. I dropped to my knees multiple times begging God to take some of my health and transfer it to my brother. I feared Iván being stuck in a vegetative state more than him dying.

I experienced an envy I never felt before as the months went by. I felt jealous of elderly people because God blessed them with decades of life while my brother barely clung onto his twenties. I lost my brother to drugs years ago long before he landed on life support. Our last time together before his traumatic brain injury was a painful experience.

I was so angry at him that I told him he was dead to me and I refused to hug him goodbye. I will *never* say this again to someone I love. Iván had been arguing with our father over prescription pills. Simply put, Iván wanted more and more. I remember seeing him standing in the kitchen. I had no idea this could have been the last time I saw him alive. I left our house full of rage, sadness, and fear. My father drove me back to Johns Hopkins University. It was a familiar drive down the same roads until my father started praying out loud.

Signs You're in Survival Mode

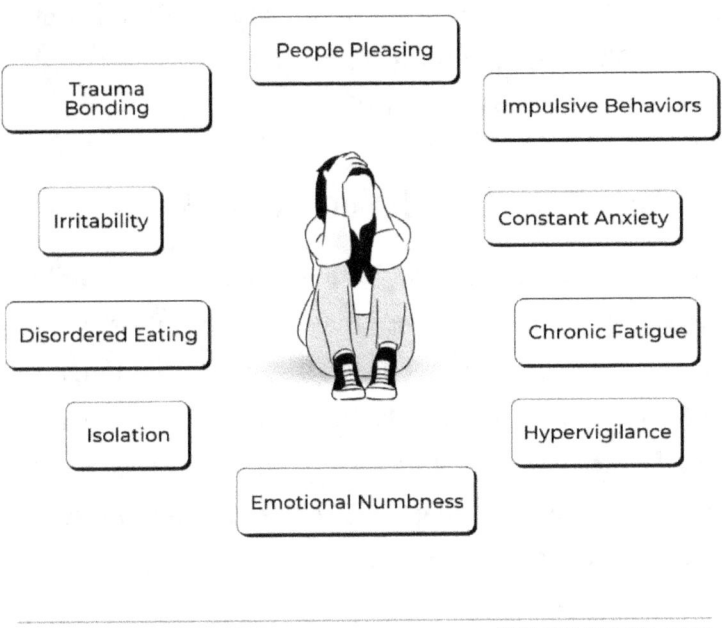

People Pleasing

Trauma Bonding

Impulsive Behaviors

Irritability

Constant Anxiety

Disordered Eating

Chronic Fatigue

Isolation

Hypervigilance

Emotional Numbness

My father is a bold and fearless man, but in this moment his vocal cords trembled with desperation and uncertainty. I listened as my father surrendered his only son to God. He told God that he didn't know what else to do. We were lost and frantic for a solution to Iván's addiction. Time would reveal that God heard us and answered our prayers that night. God's resolution was beyond our imagination.

I was in the middle of my junior year at Johns Hopkins when my brother suffered his life-threatening brain injury. I did not ask for any extensions on my assignments let alone take a day off. This is not a brag but evidence of how little boundaries and self-care I implemented in my life at the time. The unfathomable amount of stress was a ticking time bomb that eventually exploded into my life-threatening eating disorder. I graduated university with two majors and two eating disorders.

Your Body Will Tell You What It Needs

I didn't understand what an eating disorder was until I was diagnosed with one. I've learned that I met several risk factors for developing an eating disorder due to my unhealed trauma, history of weight bullying, stress, and family record of disordered eating.[5] I entered college with a battered body image after years of family members and peers insisting I was "fat" and "ugly." I internalized after countless put-downs that no matter what I did, I would be

---

[5] "Eating Disorders," Mayo Clinic, https://www.mayoclinic.org/diseases-conditions/eating-disorders/symptoms-causes/syc-20353603.

told I was fat or reminded of how I used to be fat. I engaged in emotional eating during my freshman and sophomore years of college to cope with mountaining stress.

The immense amount of powerlessness I felt over Iván's traumatic brain injury snowballed into obsessively controlling my calorie intake and workouts by my senior year of college. My meals looked more like snacks and caused me as much stress as a college exam.

I imagined running away when I would run on the treadmill but I could never outrun the pain I felt. My subconscious shift from binge drinking to binge exercising was medically unsurprising because of a strong link between disordered eating, substance abuse, and unhealed trauma.[6]

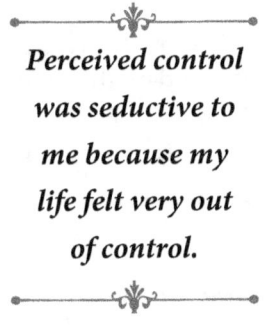

Perceived control was seductive to me because my life felt very out of control.

Perceived control was seductive to me because my life felt very out of control. I could not control my brother's addiction or if he would ever wake up from his coma. But I could control how many calories I ate and burned daily. I couldn't control what happened to my parents as kids or whether their marriage would last. But I could control how long my workouts were and the numbers on the scale. Eventually, my haggard face, underweight body, and compulsive exercise raised red flags. I credit my mother for breaking my trance. I remember her sending

---

[6] Noah Eskander et al., "The Risk of Substance Abuse Among Adolescents and Adults with Eating Disorders," *Cureus* 12, no. 9 (September 8, 2020), https://pmc.ncbi.nlm.nih.gov/articles/PMC7544549/.

me a text saying, "You look sick." Tears fell from my eyes when I read her text because I knew she was right.

Complex trauma had unlocked a new mental illness that would suck the life out of me until I nursed my core wounds. At the height of my eating disorder, I remember thinking, *I forgot how to eat.* How did I go from being a foodie to fixating on the nutritional content of a single grape? How did I go from rarely working out to doing three hours of cardio to burn off what I ate?

Ultimately, my eating disorder landed me at an eating disorder treatment center for a ten-week outpatient program. My physician wanted me to go into a residential program which is the level before hospitalization, but I was able to convince, or rather manipulate, my doctor to agree to the less intensive treatment. I couldn't fathom the idea of not working out or being immersed in a day-and-night program again.

My thought process at the time captures how compulsive my exercise was and my need to feel in control. This program involved intensive individual and group therapy, regular weigh-ins, exercise restrictions, wearing a heart monitor, and following their eating plan. I recognize the irony of the need for perceived control resulting in me enrolling into a program where I am told what to eat, how to eat, and when to step on the scale.

The hardest part of this treatment program was not the invasive assessments or the bland food we ate. It was balancing being a caretaker for my brother with healing from a psychiatric disorder with the highest mortality rate.[7] I sat in rooms where women talked about losing pregnancies, relationships, and jobs to their eating disorders. I listened as they discussed hospitalizations, permanent physical damage, and uncertain futures due to their disordered eating, or "good girl's addiction." I wish I could say I had a handle on my eating disorder when I left the program, but it was only the beginning.

My body cried out for help in other ways apart from my eating disorders. About two weeks into my brother's coma, I recall sitting in class when suddenly I thought, *It's happening.* I knew this feeling well. I felt this way outside the gas station when I was sixteen, outside a high school when I was seventeen, at the orthodontist when I was eighteen, and now in my college course at twenty. I barely walked out of the classroom and into the bathroom before I started vomiting uncontrollably. Afterward, I laid down on a bench in the lobby where I was shortly transported by campus security to the student health center.

I experienced what are known as vasovagal syncope episodes during times of heightened stress. Symptoms of my vasovagal syncope episodes include my heart rate and blood pressure suddenly dropping, a loss of strength, shaking, nausea, fear, and fainting. My junior year wouldn't be the last time I needed to be transported to receive medical attention after leaving in the middle of class. The next time would be in law school where I almost

---

[7] Nathalie Auger et al., "Anorexia nervosa and the long-term risk of mortality in women," *World Psychiatry* 23, no. 3 (September 9, 2021): 448–49, https://pmc.ncbi.nlm.nih.gov/articles/PMC8429328/.

collapsed in the front office. I had to be taken by ambulance in this case to a local emergency room.

My body tried to tell me it wasn't okay many times. Its pleas were getting harder to ignore, such as stress-induced hives, hair loss, and dissociation. I consulted with several doctors to figure out what I might be suffering from. After a battery of tests, the answer was always "stress." If my nervous system could write, it would have written a massive sign that

"What you don't repair, you repeat."

said, "What you don't repair, you repeat." I repeated cycles of pain, self-destruction, and toxicity for years after college.

I started law school about six months after completing my eating disorder treatment and being in no position to throw myself into another high-stress environment. My decision to go to law school was another form of running away. It was an act of self-harm disguised as ambition. I had not accepted yet that I could not "achieve" my way out of trauma, so I kept trying no matter the cost to my mental health. Spoiler alert: No update to my resume or additional degree made me happy.

Law school offered me stability. I knew for three years that I would have the same home, clear expectations, and structure. I was achieving the American dream and escaping the trauma I experienced in Maryland. The cherry on top was an almost full-ride scholarship to attend. I couldn't pass up the opportunity to wear a new mask—an aspiring attorney. Law school was very stressful but not "your brother is dying" stressful. My college experience raised my stress threshold to new heights, but during law school, the weight of both past and recent trauma ultimately overwhelmed my nervous system.

Wherever I went, the nightmares, stoicism, anxiety, self-sabotage, and old habits followed. Like in college, I avoided my feelings while in law school through studying, disordered eating, and partying. The bulimia and anorexia morphed into binge eating. Partying in the Hills replaced partying in the hood. I chased one temporary distraction after another, never feeling like I belonged. I had yet to understand that wanting to escape is a natural human response to pain. For example, our bodies release natural painkillers called endorphins when we accidentally sprain our ankles or burn our hands on the stove.

My self-destructive behaviors were my "painkillers." They weren't healthful or sustainable coping mechanisms but they were valid attempts to cope with hurt. It's taken years for me to not see myself as broken, "crazy," or dumb for the self-destruction I did while under the influence of trauma. I've put in countless hours to transform shame into self-compassion.

Stigma around and glamorization of substance abuse persists. What I wish more people understood is that substance abuse is like carrying a sign that says, "I'm not okay." I have not met a single person who is emotionally stable, satisfied with

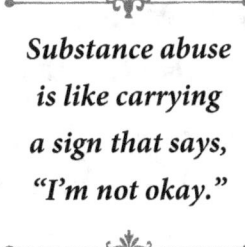

Substance abuse is like carrying a sign that says, "I'm not okay."

their life, *and* abuses substances. Abusing drugs to cope with trauma is like putting a Band-Aid on a bullet wound—ineffective and dangerous in the long-term. My mask of an ambitious aspiring attorney was slipping, and it was a matter of time before I didn't have enough energy to pretend anymore.

Substance abuse can also exacerbate mental disorder symptoms. I did not receive my borderline personality disorder or obsessive compulsive disorder diagnoses until I was in my late twenties. I wonder how my life would have been different had I received the necessary treatment and medication earlier. I had been walking a tightrope between self-destruction and survival for years. Even my attempts at self-care were at times counterproductive. For instance, the two therapists I saw during and shortly after law school caused what I now know as secondary victimization.

I learned the hard way that not putting myself first costs joy, money, time, and so much more. I needed to learn how to stop recycling and reenacting trauma. I needed to break this vicious cycle of pain for Adult Priscilla, Little Priscilla, and my future children. My inner child motivates me to prioritize myself because I cannot let her down the way so many others did.

The Mental Health Cost of Not Putting Yourself First

Imagine running a marathon with unexpected inclines and turns. Your heart is racing and your legs are begging you to quit the 26.2-mile course. Would you help your friend move out of their house or mow your elderly neighbor's lawn after crossing the finish line? The obvious answer is no due to physical exhaustion. Your body will let you know through muscle inflammation, hyperventilation, and dehydration that it needs to recover before providing physical assistance to anyone.

Why do many of us approach *emotional marathons* differently? Think of a stressful time in your life—an extended time when your sleep was compromised, your anxiety levels were unbearable, and your digestive system was distressed. Did you listen to your body's desperate pleas to pause and rest? Or did you drain yourself and pour into others at the expense of your peace and wellness? I ran emotional marathons with little to no pit stops for years until life taught me that physical and mental health are equally important.

I wish one of my physicians would have shed light on trauma or encouraged me to get screened for post-traumatic stress disorder (PTSD). Seeking support from mental health professionals was crucial to my healing journey.

Accessing professional mental health services is challenging for many people. Stigma, cost of care, language barriers, and fear are some of the barriers to therapy.

My experience as a Latina highlights how cultural stigma also hinders many from seeking therapy. Apart from my parents, therapy was not openly talked about in my family. A family member telling you to go see a therapist was often an insult or an insult disguised as a joke because it meant you were "crazy." Crazy, or *loco* in Spanish, is a pejorative term that perpetuates mental health stigma. The reality is seeking professional help takes courage and strength. Accepting support is not evidence of feebleness or cowardice. It is easier for some people to ridicule another person's healing journey than to mend their deepest wounds. Becoming the family's cycle breaker comes with a risk of becoming the family's black sheep.

Seeking professional help takes courage and strength. Accepting support is not evidence of feebleness or cowardice.

Be the Person Who Breaks the Cycle

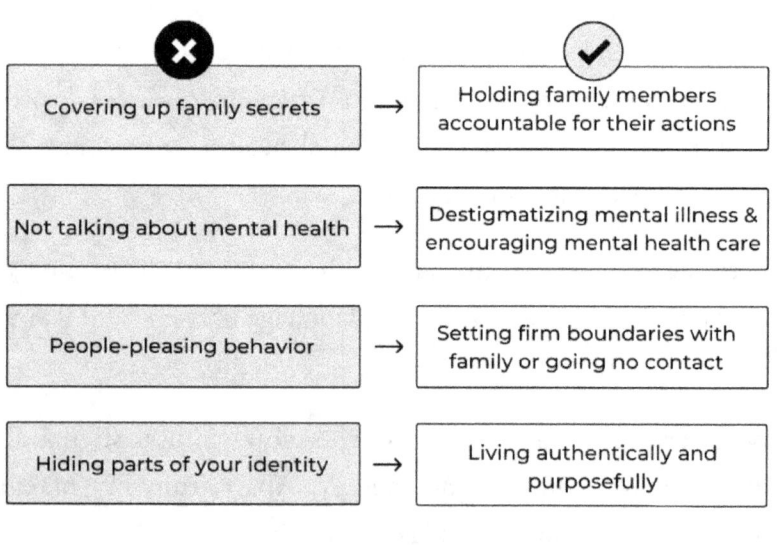

✖		✔
Covering up family secrets	→	Holding family members accountable for their actions
Not talking about mental health	→	Destigmatizing mental illness & encouraging mental health care
People-pleasing behavior	→	Setting firm boundaries with family or going no contact
Hiding parts of your identity	→	Living authentically and purposefully

Growing up I would hear disparaging and minimizing comments about mental illness like someone is *malito* (unwell) or *enfermita* (sick). *Ito* is a diminutive suffix in Spanish that makes a smaller or more affectionate version of a word. It's like adding a cherry on top of an otherwise insulting or derogatory comment. I was not the first nor will I be the last person in my family to have a mental illness. Previous generations of my family did not have the resources that I am privileged to have to receive a diagnosis, let alone treatment.

My *Abuelita* (Grandma) Bertha would describe having *nervios* or nervousness. *Nervios* is a vague blanket term for anything from situational anxiety to post-traumatic stress disorder. I used to wish as a little girl that I would see my Abuelita Bertha go a full day without crying. It made me sad and concerned to see her cry and live in constant fear of different phobias. From what I know of her life, she endured significant trauma from losing at least two children, living in poverty as a child, enduring domestic violence from my grandfather, and being married to a pedophile.

My grandmothers are a big motivation for me to practice self-care. They demonstrated that self-care does not have to be lavish or costly. Self-care can be cooking *llapingachos con fritada* (Ecuadorian potato patties with braised pork), walking to *el mercado* (the market) in the fresh air, and knitting keepsakes. Our bodies and minds need nourishment and rest. They need the ability to hit pause through mindfulness practice, movement, and connection.

Self-care helps us shift from surviving to thriving. Our phone will go "dead" or overheat if it's not charged properly. What do you think happens to your nervous system without proper care and support?

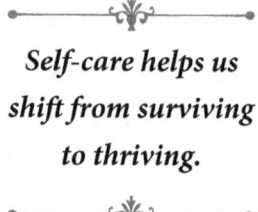

Self-care helps us shift from surviving to thriving.

Self-care is as much about learning as it is unlearning. I had to unlearn cultural messaging that didn't serve my joy, such as *La ropa sucia se lava en casa* or "dirty laundry is washed at home." Chronic stress from washing dirty laundry at home or holding secrets compromised my immune system, sleep, and overall health for years. Research shows that harboring secrets can trigger the body's stress response, leading to issues like headaches, digestive problems, and an increased risk of heart disease over time.[8] Liberation from secrets and dysfunction was an incentive for me to seek support outside the home and work with therapists.

If you broke your arm, would you ask an unlicensed friend who never went to medical school to perform surgery? The obvious answer is no because they are unqualified and could jeopardize your health. Similarly, turning to someone with no mental health licensure or specialization for your trauma healing is risky. To be clear, it can be beneficial to lean on loved ones for support whether your arm or soul needs surgery. But the actual surgery or psychological treatment should be left to the professionals.

---

[8] Ruben Castaneda, "How Your Secrets Can Damage and Maybe Even Kill You," *U.S. News & World Report*, June 26, 2017, https://health.usnews.com/wellness/mind/articles/2017-06-26/how-your-secrets-can-damage-and-maybe-even-kill-you.

Challenges can persist even after you access mental health care. Experience taught me that licensing and regulation is not enough to protect patients from problematic therapists. Prejudice and biases like racism, sexism, and xenophobia do not automatically disappear behind the doors of a therapist's office. My assumption that all therapists provide safe spaces made it harder for me to realize when a therapist crossed boundaries. Consider some of the following experiences I had inside a therapist's office.

"You don't like when people stereotype you, but you act like a stereotype," asserted Dr. Outofpocket regarding my angry moments. She also pointed out how I would "use slang" when I would get mad and "turn into another person." She was referring to the "Crazy Latina" trope that disparagingly depicts Latinas as emotionally unstable, viciously jealous, and sexual. The Crazy Latina trope adds a layer of stigma and misunderstanding for Latinas. I've heard comments from men who have made my mental health into a joke or, worse, a fetish. For instance, a former boyfriend asked me to not take my medication one time before we were going to hook up because he "wanted to see how I was without it." In other words, he wanted to see if I would be some feral nympho without medication.

I have heard similar stories from other women of color, such as those targeted by the "angry Black woman" trope. Mental illness is not a character flaw, joke, or fetish. It's a serious condition that needs to

Mental illness is not a character flaw, joke, or fetish. It's a serious condition that needs to be met with compassion.

be met with compassion. Dr. Outofpocket knew how much this stereotype bothered me because I shared how I'd been at the receiving end of jokes and judgments founded in this trope since I was a child. For instance, I've received comments like the one below under an interview I did about living with borderline personality disorder:

 **@MrHandsomeferny** 3 weeks ago
All latina women are like her lol

      Reply

Anger is a valid and healthy emotion that often signals that injustice is taking place. My rage was a natural response to the abuse I was experiencing in my relationship. No, my mistreatment does not excuse my reactive abuse. But it does add an explanation apart from me "acting like a stereotype." Dr. Outofpocket never acknowledged the influence she had on my relationship or took accountability for the times she overstepped and overshared during my therapy sessions.

I internalized Dr. Outofpocket's opinions as my own. I figured she knew best. After all, I was the "manic" one as she described me despite never offering me an official diagnosis. For example, I told her during a session that I almost gave into sex with my boyfriend even though I was not ready for that to be a part of our relationship yet. That night he went on about how stressed he was and how oral sex wasn't enough for him. He explained how us starting to have sex would give him the stress release he needed. He even worried about whether his penis would "stop working" if he didn't have sex soon.

I felt like a bad girlfriend after all he said. I told him my boundaries before we became a couple. He agreed to them. I felt pressured to, at a minimum, reconsider my boundaries. So, I did, and asked him, "Do you love me?" as I contemplated giving him the sex he wanted badly. He replied, "Wait, hold on, I'm not selling you a dream" and cut me off before I could give in. I tried to explain to him that I felt pressured by his words and actions to redact my boundaries. He said, "No, I didn't. I didn't pressure you."

When I spoke to my therapist about what happened, she criticized me for "setting him up to fail" and "testing him." She went on to say that if we had slept together, I would "forever hold it against him." I was caught off guard by her response. No fiber of me was trying to set my boyfriend up to do anything or otherwise behave manipulatively. I left the session feeling like an even worse girlfriend and confused as to why I felt pressured when my therapist painted me as a manipulator and my boyfriend completely dismissed my feelings.

Apart from overstepping boundaries regarding my relationship, Dr. Outofpocket freely disclosed information about herself that I didn't need to know from her having a breast augmentation, a "big butt" in high school, and her being raped by her husband but still staying with him. She also nicknamed me the "Disconnect Queen" because of my propensity for dissociation and told me to stop feeling sad about my brother's traumatic brain injury and instead be grateful to

God that he is alive. It's no surprise that I lost my voice years ago—I had unwillingly empowered others to silence me.

It's not "all in your head."

Unhealed trauma increases the risk of:

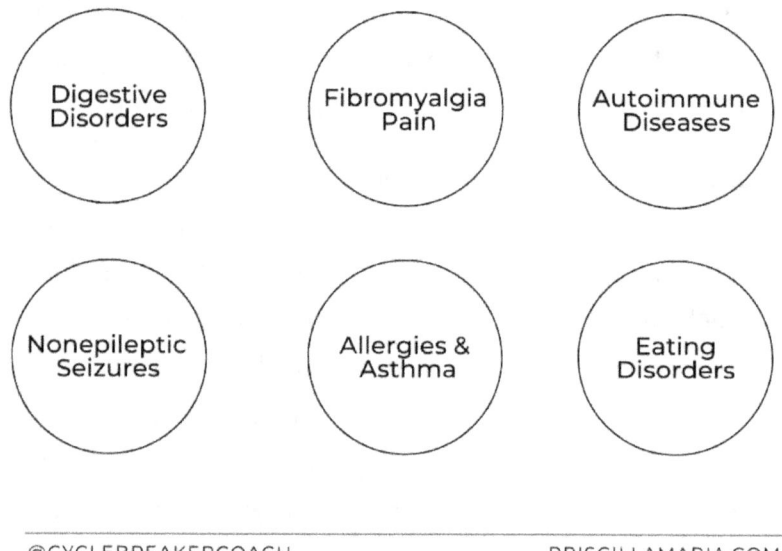

Digestive Disorders

Fibromyalgia Pain

Autoimmune Diseases

Nonepileptic Seizures

Allergies & Asthma

Eating Disorders

@CYCLEBREAKERCOACH   PRISCILLAMARIA.COM

Cultural Scripts

"Todo bien gracias a Dios" or "everything's good thanks to God" is a phrase I grew up hearing that I now know can sometimes mask the most dysfunctional family secrets. The way this phrase is used and how often it is used reflects the cultural scripts that influenced my upbringing, including *machismo, marianismo,* and *familismo.*

These cultural scripts are like deeply ingrained rules that set many of us on a trajectory that may not be in alignment with our values and ambitions. They can feel oppressive and contradictory for many of us.

According to Dr. Patricia Conde-Brooks, Executive Director of Campus Inclusion and Community at the University of St. Thomas, cultural scripts are a "pattern of interactions, shared by members of a cultural group and shaped from common experiences, by which objects and events can be identified and understood. They create a meaning system for a particular cultural group."[9] These cultural scripts can be beneficial, detrimental, or both and affect how a Latina shows up in her professional and personal life. Professionally, *familismo* can look like valuing family approval for career decisions. *Marianismo* might look like being humble and not speaking about your accomplishments at the cost of a promotion. *Machismo* might look like not fighting back when a man gets ahead despite less experience and accolades.

Marianismo is the cultural expectation that women should be self-sacrificing, nurturing, and submissive like the Virgin Mary. This concept reinforces that a woman's worth is tied to her mother-hood, marriage, and how of service she is to others. I was raised Catholic so *marianismo* and *machismo* were especially reinforced in my family system. I can recall several uncles and family friends who expected their wives to serve them and esteem them as the

---

[9] Patricia Conde-Brooks, "Recognizing La Cultura: The Experience of Cultural Scripts in Latina Leadership," Doctoral Dissertation, University of St. Thomas Minnesota, February 3, 2020, https://core.ac.uk/reader/289222420.

head of the household. Similarly, sons, especially the eldest, are often treated as kings.

This combination of scripts can look like serving a man his meal first, having him sit at the head of the table, asking permission as a woman for any decision from where to sit to if they can travel, and handling all domestic duties. I did not grow up within a *machista* household. My father did not like to be placed on a pedestal, and my mother certainly wasn't going to place him on one. For example, one time my abuela insisted my mother get up and serve my father a plate. My mother declined and insisted he could get food himself and my father agreed. I take accountability for my internalized machismo. It took me too long to value and understand how hard my mother worked as a stay-at-home mother. I mirrored what I saw: others' expectation that mothers and wives carry the domestic role.

Although I grew up in an egalitarian household, one of my parents said they couldn't treat my brother and me the same because "he's a boy and you're a girl." That meant I experienced significantly more restrictions than my brother. For example, if I felt overwhelmed with chores and school work, I might be told, "Imagine when you're a mom. You're going to be busy with everything plus kids. *No puedes tener los guambras cagados y meados* (You can't have the kids in soiled diapers)." I recall when I said I was stressed out while juggling an intensive outpatient program for my eating disorder and taking my brother to his outpatient physical rehabilitation program, I was told by a family member, "Why are you stressed? You don't pay bills. You are his sister. You are supposed to help."

I've had to unlearn several messages such as my worth being tied to how cooperative I am with others. I think of thirteen- and fourteen-year-old Priscilla who barely spoke in school. Who sat alone at lunch. Who didn't speak up when she was in a gym class of all boys who allowed her to fall to the ground during a rope course exercise. Who decided not to share about her bullying at school to her parents to not be a burden. She had learned at an even younger age that her cries for help wouldn't lead to the justice she needed.

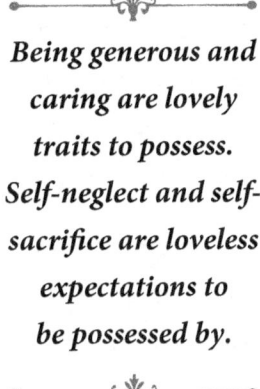

I think of adult Priscilla in a relationship who, even after her boyfriend raped her, buried what happened and helped him in writing his commencement speech for a large public university he attended. I didn't want to go but gave in. I wanted to escape but not on a flight to the Midwest to support his dreams. I swallowed the pain and went through the motions, worried what others would say.

Being generous and caring are lovely traits to possess. Self-neglect and self-sacrifice are loveless expectations to be possessed by.

Being generous and caring are lovely traits to possess. Self-neglect and self-sacrifice are loveless expectations to be possessed by. These expectations can be communicated subtly and palatably through lasting adages like, *"Calladita te ves más bonita"*—which roughly translates to "You look prettier with your mouth closed." The casual nature in which this saying is often delivered is misleading. This phrase makes clear that a modest and quiet woman is a virtuous one. It serves to police women from being outspoken, bold, or independent and to instead be compliant and subdued. Messaging from media, family, and society pushed messages that a woman's worth was tied to how she dressed, spoke, and served others.

Under a *marianismo* framework, female sexuality is dangerous. To be sensual is to risk sexual assault or a sordid reputation. I grew up with the belief that sex comes after marriage and that all heterosexual men will target you for sex. *Marianismo* encourages girls and women to be sexually abstinent and modest until marriage. I can recall several occasions where, as a child, I was taught to dress a certain way because "men will be there." Not once did I ever hear a boy or a man be told to not prey on little girls. It was implied that if a man sexually violated you, you somehow tempted them to act that way.

I have felt torn between cultural expectations and stereotypes. On one hand, old-school families demand we act modestly, while pervasive stereotypes in American society expect us to be "crazy," "spicy," and "sensual." We're expected to perform for the male gaze to find a partner but also repress our sexual expression. These black-and-white perspectives coupled with sexual trauma have made sex a stressful topic for most of my life. There's so much messaging from your father needing to "give you away" to needing to wear white on your wedding day. The whole concept of virginity complicated my self-image and self-worth. In the wilderness program when I wrote the therapeutic letter to my grandfather, I questioned what I did to cause him to be sexually attracted to me. It's heartbreaking to think that for years I felt partially responsible for my molestation because of the messaging I grew up with.

When you hear people even to this day say things like "What was she wearing?" or "She's dressed like a slut, so of course guys are going to grab her." Now, I know that there is only one cause of sexual assault and that is perpetrators. Clothing is not consent. Being in a relationship is not consent. Silence is not consent. A "yes" under duress is not consent. There was nothing sexually appealing about me as an eight- and ten-year-old. I was wearing children's clothing and very much an innocent child. A rapist is completely at fault for raping someone. Someone who is not a rapist would never rape another person, no matter the circumstances.

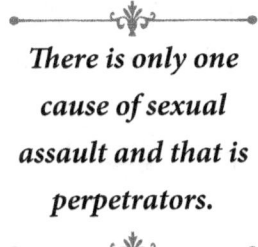

There is only one cause of sexual assault and that is perpetrators.

It's no surprise that for the majority of my life, I have blamed myself for the sexual assaults I've suffered. I also was a late bloomer when it came to identifying as bisexual. My sexuality was stunted by my Catholic upbringing, cultural messaging, and sexual trauma. Some of my elders were or are staunchly against same-sex relations and relationships. Quite literally, a heterosexual pedophile could receive more acceptance than a queer upstanding person.

I grew up being taught that ladies sat with their legs closed, didn't show their bra straps, needed to prepare for motherhood since girlhood, and always slept in their own homes.

Dating was not encouraged among female relatives, but male relatives were allowed to date, have the home to themselves, and be given much more freedom. Being at an intersection of traditional gender roles and modern expectations was confusing, to say the least. I was encouraged to pursue higher education but also taught by some elders that I needed to know how to cook, clean, and raise children to attract a husband.

Compassionate reflection has allowed me to extend grace to my female elders. Two things can be true at once: Some of my *abuelitas* and *tias* (aunts) perpetuated harmful cultural scripts that negatively impacted me and they did so with good intentions. I honor them for being cycle breakers in their own right. I recognize that they exemplified resilience for me in incredible ways. They disrupted the status quo in their worlds at the risk of being ostracized or worse so that I may live the privileged life I have today.

My Abuelita Bertha married my grandfather to be able to leave her house and later regretted marrying the first man who pursued her. My Abuelita Gloria could not go anywhere unchaperoned when she was unwed. She always needed to be in the presence of a protective man. I always grew up hearing about my grandfathers' behaviors. It was no secret that they were unfaithful, promiscuous, and fathered children with multiple women. Yet they were still revered. Their sexual history did not taint their worth or lessen their value as a potential spouse.

Core to familismo, or the cultural value that emphasizes the importance of family loyalty and support, is respecting your elders.

It is expected that you greet elders and give them deference. Even in the Spanish language, there is another word for addressing someone with respect—usted. If I did not say buenas tardes or buenas noches, I risked being reprimanded for being rude. On one hand, I put my family's needs before my own, but on the other hand I've received copious amounts of emotional, physical, and financial support from family members over the years under the same umbrella of familismo. You could see then why I was confused and hurt as a child when the respect was not mutual.

One of my grandparents would mercilessly body-shame me long before I knew what body-shaming was. I'll offer a few examples that illustrate what I endured for about a decade. When I was thirteen, I was standing next to them when they abruptly slapped my stomach and said, "No!" They did this in front of my aunt. My aunt said nothing to correct the message, so I took my grandparent's words and my aunt's lack of intervention as my body was wrong. According to this grandparent, I had a gut or *barriga* and I needed to lose weight. I heard versions of this countless times over the years when we would visit California. It's why I avoided spending time with some of my paternal family. On top of being bullied at school, I didn't want to be bullied by my elders.

When my maternal grandmother died, an elder told me, "You need to get on a treadmill. I keep telling you to lose weight!" Yes, even grief wasn't enough to get a break from body-shaming. This elder would say things like "You need to lose all that weight, you are so short,"

"You need to buy this exercise machine for your stomach," "You don't need to be ordering that," or "That's a lot of food!"

When I developed an eating disorder, I made it a point to tell this grandparent. There was a part of me that hoped this grandparent would make a connection between their words and my fractured self-image. This example should answer whether my eating disorder did anything to deter their body-shaming. When I saw them after my eating disorder treatment and once I was in law school, they looked me up and down in the living room with people around and said, "What size are you wearing now? A size 16?"

This is how they greeted me. Not a hug, not a "How's law school? Congratulations," or "I'm proud of you." But this exchange wasn't new. It had been happening since I was thirteen. I used to think that if I was skinny this elder would love me. I would work out a week before flying to Los Angeles hoping I'd shed some weight before seeing them. I didn't understand why elders could talk to us in any type of way and we had to just take it. Holding someone accountable is not disrespectful. Accurately describing someone's behavior is not disrespectful. But growing up I was taught the opposite—elders were off limits, no matter what.

Accurately describing someone's behavior is not disrespectful.

Both of my parents came from a "broken" household characterized by domestic violence, divorce, and unspeakable trauma. I saw how both of my grandfathers lacked parental involvement whereas my grandmothers picked up their slack. My paternal grandfather, for instance, would quote Scripture and become irate if anyone criticized the fact that he abandoned my father and uncles. After all, machismo and centuries of paternalism were on his side. He was a male elder and questioning him was automatically perceived by him and some as "disrespectful." Accurately describing my grandfather's parenting, or lack thereof, is not disrespectful. If he did not want that to be his legacy, he should have taken a better course of action.

The other side of *familismo* can look like ample emotional, physical, and financial support from family members often with muddled or nonexistent boundaries. Leaning on each other was necessary for survival in a new country for both sides of my family. My father lived transiently with his grandmother, mother, and two brothers for years hopping from garage to living room floor, to couch until they were eventually asked to leave. As a family, we have stayed with different relatives and vice versa. I am too young to remember when we and another family briefly lived in a two-bedroom apartment in San Bruno, California.

These cultural scripts are fueled by the subjugation of girls and women. I think of my female ancestors in Ecuador, Nicaragua, and beyond whose voices were quieted and potentials were limited and predefined. I'm happy to see my generation and younger generations openly criticize and reject antiquated gender roles. We are allowed to select what parts of our heritage we want to pass along. Throughout my life, I have moved and expressed myself cautiously. I consciously and subconsciously followed the roles I inherited via tradition. I think of the many times I've shortchanged myself professionally to not be perceived as too demanding or arrogant. I've had to deconstruct messages about *Latinidad* and liberate myself from the tug-of-war between cultural expectations and popular stereotypes.

Adolescent Priscilla motivates me to stay curious and audacious when it comes to tradition. She was always quiet in school because she saw academics as a job. She didn't want to be loud or misbehave and completely bought into *marianismo*. Her fourth-grade teacher nicknamed her the "Mother Teresa" of the class, eager to help others even at the expense of getting her work done. At the same time, she was treated unfairly by some teachers and perceived to be whatever they thought a Latina was—from being told to "calm down" or that her tone was "nasty" in middle school to being falsely accused of skipping class in high school.

> *We are fully capable of authoring our stories and not being passive characters in someone else's prewritten story.*

I had to find and reclaim my voice that wasn't allowed to properly blossom. The more I invalidate outdated cultural pressures, the more I validate my experience and self-worth. I no longer play small. I am not a bland piece of bread to be digestible. I am a cycle breaker with many layers and flavors and so are you. We are fully capable of authoring our stories and not being passive characters in someone else's prewritten story. We don't need to make ourselves small or otherwise sacrifice our authenticity to make someone else feel more comfortable.

You Are the Expert on Your Body and Experiences

Nobody is *qualified* to judge you. Nobody can accurately determine your worth or potential. Nobody has worn your shoes and walked each step you have. You are the artist and the canvas. Don't accept someone's misinterpretation of the art that is you as law. I have never met a judgmental person who is not a hypocrite. A judgmental person gets a break from their internal shame every time they criticize someone else. In a world pulsating with unsolicited opinions, a cycle breaker can filter out the noise and lean into their intuition and knowledge.

A judgmental person gets a break from their internal shame every time they criticize someone else.

Identifying as the expert on your body and experiences is an act of empowerment. This declaration establishes you as the authority on your wellness and dethrones anyone from dictating your story. Your opinion of yourself towers over external validation and you hold the title as the best advocate for your dreams and healing. This identity is essential to cycle-breaking and is made possible through authenticity and a robust self-validation muscle. My journey as a mental health patient serves as a cautionary tale about the hazards of not standing firmly in your expertise. I was raised to respect authority figures and elders. Accordingly, I trusted each therapist, psychiatrist, and mental health professional with my deepest wounds because of the degrees and clinical hours they completed.

Looking back I realize that several of the mental health professionals I worked with acted inappropriately. I'll include some examples so that you and others can pick up on the red flags I missed. I was about seventeen years old when I worked with my first therapist. She gathered detailed information during our first session about my history and current circumstances to build a treatment plan. A common topic covered in a therapy intake is your trauma history.

I disclosed my molestation and her response was, "Was he senile?" I'm unsure as to why that was her immediate response. My grandfather did not live with dementia or any similar cognitive condition. He was a pedophile who preyed on little girls. What I needed at that moment was to be believed and comforted, not to be presented with a possible excuse for deplorable behavior. She would often look at her nails or out the window during our sessions. I felt like I was boring her. I wish I could say she was the only therapist I had that would read texts during sessions.

The therapists I worked with in California and Michigan caused me the most harm. I reached out to these therapists under the heaviness of fear, desperation, and emotional dysregulation. I also was limited to a provider who was covered by my insurance and who didn't have a long waiting list. The comments they made are difficult to describe because they reveal intimate details of my traumas. I stayed in these therapeutic relationships because I couldn't get an outside opinion without disclosing my traumas. There were no checks and balances inside their offices. Their comments fell into several categories: victim-blaming, invalidation, and outright profanity.

When I told Dr. Outofpocket my partner pushed me, she told me she was surprised it hadn't happened sooner. I felt foolish when I confided in her about blocking my room door with a suitcase to feel safer in a house where an elderly man was staying as well. Instead of affirming my PTSD symptoms, she scoffed at my fear with, "Oh because the suitcase is really going to stop someone from coming in." Dr. Outofpocket is part of the reason I stayed in my toxic relationship.

Finding a mental health professional you are compatible with takes patience, effort, and time. The trial-and-error process is worth it when you do find someone you can open up to and feel safe with. My current therapist is Latina. She is the first Latina therapist I have ever worked with and can switch to Spanish without translating. She understands cultural expectations, taboos, and norms within our community without me having to explain them.

She does not judge me, cuss at me, or make insensitive comments when I share my experiences. She speaks to me with compassion and encourages me to do the same. Her response is far different from previous therapists who told me I would go to jail, made "jokes" about me killing someone, criticized my use of slang, or inserted details of what *they think* happened during my traumatic event. I can express myself verbally and viscerally freely unlike in other therapy sessions. For example, I would cover my face when crying in front of others out of discomfort. Dr. Outofpocket scolded me, saying "Stop covering your face!" I felt like I had done something wrong or wasn't being vulnerable enough for her approval.

Another therapist I met in California in between these therapists left me stunned by her unprofessionalism. Despite me talking about my eating disorder, she proceeded to tell me about her Weight Watchers journey, how many points certain foods were, and how hard it is to lose weight. She also felt the need to introduce me to her much younger boyfriend who was working in a back office after our session. Meeting him had nothing to do with the support I desperately needed. I only met her once and had the courage to continue my search elsewhere.

I view these younger versions of myself with compassion. She truly tried her best in therapy and thought she was being cared for by trustworthy professionals. I now have standards in place and red flags to watch out for when selecting a therapist. I encourage everyone to have clear nonnegotiables and standards within any relationship, especially one with a medical professional where your well-being is on the line.

Personal Growth and Continuous Learning

They say hindsight is 20/20. I can retrospectively see how some moments of rejection were redirection and how some people were there for a reason, season, or lesson. But at the time, I didn't see things so clearly. I've learned to trust the process and see the glass half full. When I started this journey, I thought it would be more of filling out a checklist. I anticipated that after a certain amount of therapy sessions my psychological wounds would be bandaged up and I'd become untethered to my trauma. This hasn't been the case for me.

I consider myself *healing*—not healed—because a healing journey is ongoing and nonlinear. PTSD, like other chronic health conditions, requires long-term management to reduce "flare-ups." I know that without therapy, medication, and coping strategies my mental disorder symptoms will exacerbate. Apart from these measures, I invest in personal enrichment, such as literature, events, and community groups, to promote my healing. I still spend a good amount of time consuming mindless content, but I balance it with reading books on healing complex trauma, listening to relevant podcasts, and immersing myself in supportive spaces because knowledge is revolutionary.

I found books like Natalie Gutiérrez's *The Pain We Carry* eye-opening because they explained why my body reacted the way it did to certain situations and people. My experiences had names like "triggers," "nervous system dysregulation," and "complex trauma," which were far more helpful than being called "ghetto" or *loca (crazy)*. Visit www.priscillamaria.com/author for a list of recommended books, podcasts, organizations, and documentaries to lean into.

I also learned that I was far from alone on my recovery journey. I've been able to connect to people globally who understand me. Universal themes like fear, rejection, joy, and belonging unite us regardless of our unique life stories. Meeting other survivors in communities who accept the *real* me is healing. Fellowship allows me to gain perspectives outside my internal echo chamber and acquire new coping skills, resources, and mindset shifts.

Consider the pyramids of Giza that were built by approximately 100,000 workers stone by stone over a span of decades.

These incredible pyramids were only possible through group effort. Likewise, the dream life you want to build requires community and reaching one goal after the other.

The pyramids' architects created a blueprint for skilled workers to follow. Goal-setting is a blueprint for your ideal lifestyle because it helps you track your progress, stay accountable, maintain focus, and take control.

As with any journey, you are bound to get lost without direction. Be patient and bear in mind that there is no deadline for your transformation. You are behind the wheel and set the pace. As the driver, you can *There is no deadline for your transformation.* reflect and change course accordingly. For instance, someone working toward sobriety may discover that their transformation goes beyond substance usage.

Their relationships, hangout spots, and thought patterns will likely change to achieve and sustain sobriety. Each decision they make along the way is an opportunity to learn, grow, and evolve.

Summary and Self-Care
Recap:

> *"You cannot shame yourself into change. You can only love yourself into evolution."*
>
> ~ DR. JAMES ROUSE

Challenge the Cultural Scripts You Grew Up With

➤ Adjust or discard cultural norms that do not align with your core values and beliefs.

➤ Challenge any traditional gender roles that do not serve your joy.

➤ Break any silence around mental health issues in your family by speaking openly about mental health care.

Advocate Zealously for Your Mental Wellness

➤ Seek professional help proactively as an act of self-love and strength.

➤ Pour into your mental and physical health generously and equally.

➤ Actively participate in the deconstruction of mental health stigmatization in your greater community.

Flex Your Self-Validation Muscle

➤ Lean into your intuition and cultivate your self-trust.

➤ Honor yourself as the leading authority on your body and experiences by setting boundaries and prioritizing your well-being.

➤ Practice accepting your experiences, identities, and beliefs as valid and worthy.

Commit to Continuous Personal Growth

➤ Set and pursue goals that prompt you to self-reflect and evolve.

➢ Nurture your resilience with the wisdom of your mentors and loved ones.

➢ Embrace lifelong learning through open-mindedness, accountability, and humility.

Cycle Breaker Challenge: The Write Way to Heal

Revisit to Repair

We cannot rewrite how our childhoods unfolded. What we can do is acknowledge our childhood experiences, process unresolved emotions, and hold space for transformation through inner child work. One way to reparent your inner child is through letter writing. Start by choosing a comfortable space where you can allow thoughts and feelings to flow. Select a childhood memory that left an emotional footprint on your mind and soul. I recommend choosing a memory that is not overwhelming or could trigger a flashback. Pay attention to your nervous system. It will tell you if the memory you selected is too intense. Call or text 988 if at any point you need mental health support.

Start to draft a letter after reflecting on this childhood memory. You can address the letter to your childhood self or a family member. Some ideas for your letter include expressing support and love to your younger self and advocating for their justice and well-being. Offer your inner child what they needed in that moment. Release into words whatever your body has been holding onto since this memory formed. It all belongs. This letter is for your eyes only unless you would like to share it with someone.

Take the Wheel

Take an inventory of the cultural expectations that have shaped your life. Highlight the ones that you feel restricted by. Describe how you would redefine or replace each highlighted cultural expectation. Remember this is your mental playground and you make the rules. Give yourself license to challenge tradition as you see fit and take action accordingly.

Be the Spark

It takes one cycle breaker to inspire change in a family. Documenting your mental health journey is one way to ignite interest and support for mental health in your community. There is no rush to share. What you share, how you share, who you share with, and if you share at all are completely up to you. Some ways to chronicle your

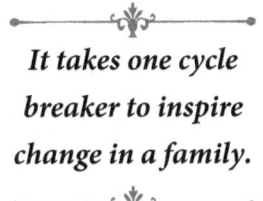

It takes one cycle breaker to inspire change in a family.

mental health journey include journaling, video diaries, songwriting, and artwork. Consider sharing with a loved one or support group whenever you feel ready. Your vulnerability could be the aspirin to someone else's pain.

Believe and Achieve

According to University of Colorado at Boulder researchers, when a person imagines a threat and when a person experiences a threat activates similar regions of the brain.[10] These findings suggest that imagination can be an effective treatment tool for phobias and post-traumatic stress. Visualization is powerful.

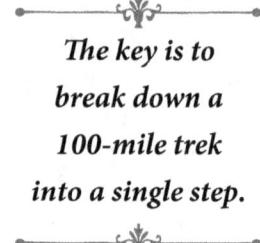

The key is to break down a 100-mile trek into a single step.

Envision what you would like to achieve in the next six months of your life. Reverse engineer your life from what you visualized through the steps below. The key is to break down a 100-mile trek into a single step. Open your notebook and declare your achievement in six months. For instance, "I am proud of myself for volunteering once a week for the last six months." Below are prompts that you could answer to reverse engineer your achievement:

➤ What boundaries, habits, and other steps did you take to achieve this goal?

➤ Who did you turn to for support?

➤ What thoughts and behaviors did you let go of?

Use these answers to create a timeline with clear milestones to outline the path it will take to achieve your goal.

---

[10] "Your brain on imagination: it's a lot like reality, study shows," University of Colorado at Boulder, Science Daily, December 18, 2018, https://www.sciencedaily.com/releases/2018/12/181210144943.htm.

PART 3
BECOME A
CYCLE BREAKER

―᠑᠑᠑᠑᠆

Family Secrets

"You should just ask her." My therapist told me this when I expressed that I suspected my grandfather had preyed on additional family members. I took her advice and reached out to one of my cousins. Let's call her Yomara.* I remember sitting on the bedroom floor of the apartment I lived in at the time bracing myself for whatever information I would hear. My heart sank when she told me, "I thought it hadn't happened to you." She continued, "You spoke so nicely of him when you gave your eulogy at his funeral." I mentally went back to that August day in 2004 after Yomara said that.

I remember standing at the podium and saying, "He taught me how to be polite and a good person." Originally I had written, "He wasn't a perfect person. He used to drink and hit my grandmother. But I still loved him." Family members discouraged me from saying these words. So I stood and said words I didn't mean in between tears. I remember sobbing once I returned to the pew but not understanding *why* I was so overcome with emotion.

My mind then wandered to a memory from when I was ten years old sitting at the top of my house's staircase. I thought to myself, *I wouldn't cry if he died. I'd only cry because Mami would be sad.* I couldn't sleep because his room was adjacent to my bedroom. How could I sleep peacefully? I was told to "lock my door at night" and would hear him kick in his sleep during nightmares. Yet, three years later, there I was, crying intensely at his funeral. In retrospect, I have a better understanding of what I was mourning, and it wasn't entirely his death. I was mourning the fact that I would never get an apology from him. I was grieving the fact that he would never be held accountable for what he did to me. Little Priscilla was weeping over things she could not put into words but felt deeply. She had not processed her molestation at her grandfather's hands. She still bought into what an elder told her after she bravely disclosed his abuse—"That wasn't molestation."

Someone disagreeing on what happened *to me* would become a familiar occurrence in my adolescence and adulthood. Invalidation from others fueled inner turmoil that led me to distrust my discernment. I learned to instead acquiesce to others' perspectives and even protect my perpetrator in some instances. My truth and need for closure became hidden beneath the weight of *familismo* and *marianismo.*

I snapped out of my memories and returned to my conversation with my cousin Yomara. She informed me that my grandfather had molested her multiple times and that his pedophilia was an "open secret." Furthermore, Child Protective Services (CPS) removed my grandfather from my aunt's Los Angeles home in the mid-90s. He was removed because Yomara had disclosed to her physician that she had been molested as a child. She was an adult at this time but her brother was a minor and still living at home with our grandfather. You might be wondering where my grandfather went after being removed by CPS. An elderly man who didn't speak English and had a limited network didn't have many options.

Perhaps the risk of homelessness is why my aunts felt it best to not tell my parents about my grandfather's removal or that he had molested Yomara. I couldn't tell you for sure. At the time, we lived in San Mateo, California, in a small two-bedroom apartment. My brother and I shared a bunk bed.

We received government assistance and support from local charities. Despite the limited space and resources, my parents generously opened up their home out of love for my grandfather. We all loved him. He was charismatic, hilarious, and fun to be around. My parents had no idea that he posed such a serious threat to me and possibly my brother.

Yomara and I had fallen victim to a cover-up in our family. *Who else had he abused?* My mind raced with questions I knew I likely would never receive answers to. I felt like I was sinking into the floor I sat on as my circle of trust shrank with each revelation. I promptly reached out to my aunts about their complicity. One aunt never replied, another aunt said my grandfather was a "good man" and "never hurt us," and the other aunt apologized for her role but falsely stated that she told my mother about the CPS removal. The aunt who apologized shared other disturbing information about my grandfather and his pedophilic track record. He was a serial child predator who not only abused children sexually but also physically abused my grandmother and verbally abused my uncle. *Why on earth was this monster allowed around us? Why was I taught to respect him and honor him as my elder?*

Growing up I was not allowed to sleep over at friends' homes and could only visit their homes if their mothers were present because of the risk of being sexually preyed on. The concept that a safe man was the exception was ingrained into my psyche as a child. You can imagine how confused I was when, in the end, the "boogeyman" was my grandfather whom I loved, and not a male classmate, neighbor, or friend's father.

The cover-up of my grandfather's pedophilia is one of many secrets in my family. My objective is not to write a tell-all book; it's to share enough detail for others to relate to and be inspired to take healing action because secrets are not unique to my family. I am now in a place where I hold compassion for my family members and accept that their actions are not excusable but explainable. Cycle-breaking is hard work. It is easier for some to look the other way or to ostracize the whistle blower than to acknowledge their involvement or confront their traumas.

Many truths remain sealed in a family vault that will likely never be released. These unspoken facts are ominous shadows. I don't know what lurks but the uneasiness persists in my family tree nonetheless. Concealment of family secrets misled me to believe that only people who aren't related to me could seriously harm me. After all, The *familismo* I grew up with reinforced that family is paramount and I could "only trust family."

Cycle-breaking is hard work. It is easier for some to look the other way or to ostracize the whistle blower than to acknowledge their involvement or confront their traumas.

My conversation with Yomara marked a turning point in my life. I didn't know how yet, but I was determined to break free from the family dynamics that empowered a pedophile to harm children without recourse. A cycle breaker is willing to endure temporary discomfort instead of a lifetime of dysfunction. They do not gloss over trauma or pass off the healing work for another generation to unpack entirely.

A cycle breaker is willing to endure temporary discomfort instead of a lifetime of dysfunction.

I also felt a sense of validation from my talk with Yomara. Someone not speaking to another relative for years over a minor disagreement was not unheard of in my family. Instead, assertive and honest conversations were often unheard.

Eventually, I learned some of the backstories behind the aggression, discord, and grudges I witnessed between family members growing up. Children are very intuitive and some of the most honest people I've met. I encourage you to reflect on any feelings you experienced as a child through inner child work. It may offer you the insight and clarity you are seeking.

Being a Cycle Breaker

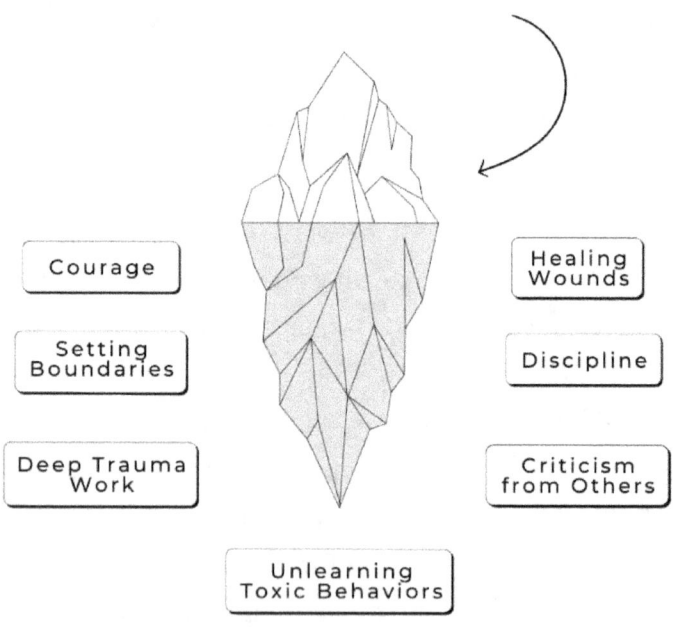

Courage

Healing Wounds

Setting Boundaries

Discipline

Deep Trauma Work

Criticism from Others

Unlearning Toxic Behaviors

Domestic Violence and Addiction

Millions of people are affected by addiction and domestic violence every year.[11] Domestic violence is an umbrella term for a variety of behaviors abusers use to assert dominion and control over victims. Perpetrators use emotional, psychological, physical, and financial violence to trap their victims in a recurring cycle of tension building, a

Domestic violence is a family infection, and the cure is a mix of education, resources, and compassion.

violent episode, and a honeymoon phase. Domestic abuse creates an environment of fear, control, and secrecy for the entire family.

According to the National Latin@ Network, one in three Latinas in America experience domestic violence during their lifetime. Many of my elders grew up witnessing their mothers endure physical abuse at the hands of their fathers. Without intervention, domestic violence can persist generationally, especially when nonphysical forms of abuse are unaddressed. Consequently, the bar for acceptable behavior can be set dangerously low in a household. For example, one of my aunts protects my abusive and philandering grandfather's legacy by insisting he was a "good man" because he never murdered anyone. Another aunt justifies her marriage to an abusive man by citing that he doesn't "cheat on her." Domestic violence is a family infection, and the cure is a mix of education, resources, and compassion.

---

[11] "Domestic Violence Statistics," National Domestic Violence Hotline, https://www.thehotline.org/stakeholders/domestic-violence-statistics/.

Addiction, like domestic violence, affects millions of people annually and can have fatal consequences.[12] Drugs are alluring for many reasons. I've heard people cite various effects of drugs that keep them coming back, such as immediate feelings of confidence, euphoria, and calmness. When I see someone dependent on drugs, I see it as a cry for help, not a reason to judge them. Mind-altering substances, in my opinion, are valid forms of coping. They are often dangerous and unsustainable forms of coping, but they are valid. Drugs provide a temporary escape from pain and worries. Someone might take Tylenol for temporary relief from arthritis. No, it does not cure arthritis but it does alleviate symptoms. It is a human instinct to avoid pain.

I was not ridiculous or wrong for the times I tried to escape emotional pain. Turning to alcohol and self-destructive behaviors to escape, however, was not the healthiest choice. Unlike Tylenol, a drug like fentanyl has a high overdose rate and can rapidly derail someone's health, career, and relationships. The reality about most drugs is that, sooner or later, the novelty wears off and consequences set in. For some, alcohol eases their anxiety; however, with time alcohol can exacerbate underlying mental health conditions, disrupt the brain's reward center, and slow down the central nervous system.

Alcohol is readily available in public and private spaces. Its accessibility is misleading and not a reflection of the dangers it poses. Part of being a cycle breaker is practicing self-awareness regardless of group thought. Ample studies support the long-term

---

[12] "Alcohol and Drug Abuse Statistics" (Facts About Addiction), American Addiction Centers, Updated March 26, 2025, https://americanaddictioncenters.org/rehab-guide/addiction-statistics-demographics.

consequences of alcohol on our organs, decision-making, and mind. Yet, alcohol remains the most used addictive substance in the country. Almost 30 million people ages twelve and older live with alcohol use disorder in the United States.[13]

If someone offered you a shiny piece of jewelry that was in demand for free would you wear it? What if that piece of jewelry included a chance of not remembering things you said or did? What if the piece of jewelry caused permanent bodily damage? What if wearing this jewelry could cost you your closest relationships? Is the dopamine rush of enjoying this jewelry and fitting in with others worth the risks? Replace shiny jewelry with a shiny bottle of alcohol and answer the same questions. Did your answers change? Let's take a deeper dive into why some use drugs despite the widely recognized risks and consequences.

According to The National Institute on Alcohol Abuse and Alcoholism, cultural stressors and socioeconomic factors contribute to elevated rates of substance abuse.[14] In Latin communities, overdose deaths have almost tripled since 2011.[15] There are several barriers to addressing drug addiction in the Latin community, including cultural, religious, and language ones. *Familismo* encourages limiting

---

[13] "Prevalence of Past-Year Alcohol Use Disorder (AUD)," NIH, updated September 2024, https://www.niaaa.nih.gov/alcohols-effects-health/alcohol-topics/alcohol-facts-and-statistics/alcohol-use-disorder-aud-united-states-age-groups-and-demographic-characteristics.

[14] Amanda Cerreto, "What to Know About Substance Abuse and the Latinx Community," UTSA, January 3, 2022, https://hcap.utsa.edu/news/2022/01/what-to-know-about-substance-use-and-the-latinx-community.html.

[15] Juliana Jiménez, "Latinos . . . overdose deaths are skyrocketing," NBC News, March 23, 2023, https://www.nbcnews.com/news/latino/drug-overdose-deaths-latinos-almost-tripled-decade-rcna76315.

discussions about domestic violence and addiction to inside the household, if these topics are spoken about at all.

Although a survivor wants to protect themselves and seek justice, the family unit might view their actions as betrayal. For instance, involving law enforcement could jeopardize the ability of undocumented family members in the household to remain in the States. I speak from experience when I say the following: Give yourself permission to step outside of your family to receive support for domestic violence.

Give yourself permission to step outside of your family to receive support for domestic violence.

Latin families can break cycles of generational trauma by:

- Not using verbal and physical violence to "discipline" children

- Not assigning children adult responsibilities, such as parenting other siblings

- Not teaching children "what happens in this house, stays in this house"

- Not pressuring children to pursue a career the family deems "acceptable"

For instance, I am the Florida State representative for Survivors for Justice Reform, a global coalition for survivors to define and achieve their definition of justice.

Machismo also contributes to underreporting and under-supporting within many Latin households. A *machista* society promotes male aggression, dominance, and stoicism. Consequently, a great number of Latino boys and men are unable to express their pain from the elevated rates of Adverse Childhood Experiences, or ACEs, they suffer compared to their non-Hispanic white peers. Toxic cycles feed into each other as studies show a strong link between ACE scores and substance abuse. Language barriers, limited access to culturally competent resources, higher rates of not being insured, and systemic inequity are additional obstacles many Latin people face in America. Breaking cycles of trauma requires change at the individual, community, and systemic levels.

No One Is Born Empty-Handed

The topic of inheritance usually centers on finances. Some of us were brought up with a silver spoon, others a plastic spork, and many of us were raised somewhere in between. I argue that, regardless of socioeconomic status, no one is born empty-handed. We come into this world with an ancestral inheritance consisting of generational gifts and traumas. Cycle-breaking is not exclusively about rehabilitating pain. Creating healthier norms also involves optimizing ancestral genius. Examples of generational gifts include resilience, talents, healing rituals, and wisdom.

Recognizing the duality of an ancestral inheritance is important. We are all repeating or breaking cycles of generational patterns. Some of the gifts I inherited include brilliance, compassion, creativity, fortitude, and humor. I can track my tenacity and fearlessness back to my father and my empathy and creativity back to my mother. On the other hand, I inherited a tendency toward forming dysfunctional relationships with people and negative coping behaviors from both sides of the family.

> No one is born empty-handed. We each inherit generational trauma and gifts.
>
> Disinheriting trauma is just as important as claiming our gifts.

GENERATIONAL TRAUMA

- Addiction
- Approval Seeking
- Codependency
- Domestic Violence
- Untreated Mental Illness

GENERATIONAL GIFTS

- Courage
- Creativity
- Wisdom
- Resilience
- Talent

As the saying goes, "To understand the present, we must first know the past." Take a moment to reflect on what familial inheritance you have been carrying and what parts you would like to disinherit. Identification of your generational traumas may not be obvious. For many of us, generational trauma may be described as,

"This is just how we are." Racialized trauma expert Resmaa Menakem said, "Trauma decontextualized in a person looks like personality. Trauma decontextualized in a family looks like family traits. Trauma decontextualized in people looks like culture."[16] Breaking a cycle of dysfunction disguised as culture and personality traits is a complex but achievable task. Disinheritance of generational toxicity might include therapy, support groups, cultural or spiritual rituals, and radical acceptance.

Metaphorically, we are passed a book of our family's saga when we enter this world. Breaking cycles is like grabbing a pen and turning into an editor. You are allowed to write new chapters and take control of your legacy according to your values. Cycle-breaking is not about rewriting history because the past is unchangeable. It's about

> *Breaking a cycle of dysfunction disguised as culture and personality traits is a complex but achievable task.*

acknowledging what happened, understanding the context in which it happened, and having the agency to harness generational wisdom and release generational trauma. The choice is yours.

Agency over Inheritance

Most things in life are outside of our control starting at birth. We can't choose our biological family, place of birth, or genetics. Our

---

[16] Resmaa Menakem, "How Do We Heal?" *Talk Easy* (podcast), November 15, 2020, https://talkeasypod.com/resmaa-menakem/.

genetic legacy is outside of our control, but what we choose to do with the cards we are dealt is within our control. Generational wealth is not just land inheritance, financial assets, and stock portfolios. Generational wealth is also core values, support, coping skills, and wellness. Generational wealth is filtering out what serves us from what holds us back. Agency is about recognizing our history and acknowledging that we do not have to be bound to repeat it or be limited by it.

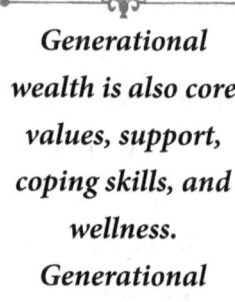

Generational wealth is also core values, support, coping skills, and wellness. Generational wealth is filtering out what serves us from what holds us back.

Consider my Abuelita Bertha and mother's experiences. My Abuelita Bertha lost her fifteen-year-old son, Jorge, in a fatal workplace accident while pregnant with my mother. I don't doubt that the extreme stress of losing a child coupled with unhealed trauma from an abusive marriage and unstable childhood, affected the in-utero environment for my mother.

According to trauma expert Mark Wolynn, a grandmother's stress can affect not only the child in her womb but her future granddaughter as well. In his book *It Didn't Start with You*, Wolynn explains how generational trauma and stress can leave a lasting imprint on DNA for generations. Studies show that a mother's stress during pregnancy can transfer to her unborn child.[17] This could

---

[17] "The In Utero Experience," ACT Government Community Services, https://www.act. gov.au/__data/assets/pdf_file/0004/2380459/The-in-utero-experience-web.pdf.

make the child more vulnerable to mental health and behavioral issues later in life. Wolynn also explains that trauma can be transmitted to children and grandchildren at a biological level through epigenetics, or the study of how environmental and behavioral factors can affect how genes function.[18]

Genetics go beyond physical traits like eye color or a propensity for cancer. Wolynn encourages readers to be curious about their emotional lineage and open to the idea that some of their fears and anxieties originated with someone else. For instance, I have carried my father's financial trauma in my body for the majority of my life despite my suburban upbringing.

I recall standing in my pantry as a high school student worried that if we didn't watch our spending we would run out of food. My father had been laid off and I was concerned that we would end up broke. I thought this as I stood inside one of the nicest houses in my neighborhood. Additionally, up until my thirties, I lived very frugally. Most of my clothing and belongings have been second-hand. I hadn't realized how many cycles of financial trauma I was repeating despite growing up financially privileged. I eventually realized that I had internalized my father's catastrophic thinking around finances. I was raised to not only consider the worst-case scenario but to always prepare for it. Waiting for the other shoe to drop, or rather for my world to turn upside down, is not a fulfilling way to live.

[18] Mark Wolynn, *It Didn't Start with You: How Inherited Family Trauma Shapes Who We Are and How to End the Cycle* (Penguin, 2016), 29–39.

I also inherited a fear and distrust toward men from both sides of my family. I didn't have a close friendship with a man until I was in law school and met my best friend, James Altamirano. I wonder how many friendships I may have missed out on because that person was a man or how many experiences I passed on because I was penny-pinching unnecessarily due to my unresolved traumas.

I am thankful for my awareness and will continue to detangle threads of trauma for my sake and the sake of future generations. I do not want to pass down these and other distorted thoughts and behavior patterns to my children. Yes, I want them to be cautious around others and fiscally responsible, but I do not want them to, like I did, see the world through the lens of constant cynicism. No, it didn't start with me but it can end with me. I can model shattering cycles of trauma unapologetically. You and I both.

Become a Cycle Creator

Generational wealth is not exclusively about breaking cycles of trauma. The other half is creating cycles of generational gifts. Take the reins and create new traditions founded on empowerment, integrity, compassion, and healing. Anything harmful that runs in your family can run out with you. Stated simply, whatever you water will grow. You can plant and water seeds of healing and authenticity that will enhance your life and the life of future generations. Whether other family members join you is outside of your control. Setting a precedent for joy, unity, and positivity is within your control.

Generational Wealth

isn't just:	it's also:
• Investing in real estate	• Healing yourself
• Purchasing life insurance	• Refusing to keep secrets
• Starting a business	• Respecting boundaries
• Contributing to a 401(k)	• Prohibiting abuse/violence
• Setting up a trust	• Teaching coping skills

@CYCLEBREAKERCOACH   PRISCILLAMARIA.COM

Creating cycles is not limited to your family of origin. This practice can apply to your community and chosen family. Here are some ways to become an architect of the future and a cycle creator:

➤ **Start New Traditions:** Have you noticed any customs in your family that are not in alignment with your values or conducive to authentic connection? For instance, how necessary is alcohol at a toddler's birthday party? You have the agency to change the status quo with positive patterns. Instead of a party centered on alcohol consumption, you might host a monthly family potluck with whomever you consider family and encourage light-hearted, inclusive discussion free of substances.

➤ **Optimize Generational Gifts:** What qualities and aspects of your family heritage are you most proud of inheriting?

Tap into and harness these qualities. You can connect with healers from your lineage who you may not know of. For instance, the majority of my ancestry is from Indigenous people in the Americas. I do not know of every single Indigenous ancestor I have, but know enough history to confidently say that my lineage is rich with resilience and creativity. Guided ancestral meditation and reading about your culture's history may help you connect with and leverage your generational gifts.

➢ **Open Lines of Communication:** Be a role model for emotional safety, respectful conflict resolution, and vulnerable communication in your family and community. You can develop the necessary skills to exemplify these practices through education and partnering with mental health professionals. Opening lines of communication can include sharing mental health resources, exemplifying self-care like journaling, or letting a loved one know that it's okay to cry and feel sad.

Summary and Self-Care

Recap:

"The wound is the place where the light enters you."

~ RUMI

Acknowledge Family Secrets and Dysfunction

➤ Recognize to the best of your ability what generational cycles of trauma are being recycled in your family.

➤ Consider what healing action you would like to take for yourself and others.

➤ Prepare yourself with mental health tools and resources for possible backlash from family members.

➤ Spread awareness of generational trauma to disrupt its circulation.

Violate Any Gag Order on Generational Cycles of Trauma

➤ Educate yourself on how family dynamics can affect a person's self-image and life trajectory through resources.

➤ Be the lighthouse in someone else's storm by offering guidance and exemplifying self-development.

➤ Confront truths in your family however is best for your wellness whether through dialogue, boundaries, or both.

➤ Encourage accountability and transparency among family members.

Exercise Your Right to Disinherit Toxic Patterns

➤ Lean into your power as a cycle breaker to change the narrative.

➤ Reflect and establish what your values and perspectives are.

> ➤ Prioritize your healing and growth through radical self-care and compassion.

> ➤ Discern and leverage the generational gifts of your lineage such as resilience or creativity.

Stay Motivated on This Marathon

> ➤ Remind yourself of what is at stake for you and future generations if harmful patterns are not addressed.

> ➤ Equip yourself with a support system that understands the importance of creating healthy patterns.

> ➤ Implement wisdom and strategies from trauma experts like those included in Mark Wolynn's *It Didn't Start with You*.

> ➤ Approach this emotional marathon with a growth mindset and go at a pace that is gentle to your body, mind, and spirit.

Cycle Breaker Challenge: Break the Silence to Break the Cycle

It is a privilege to be able to trace back your ancestry. Many people are unable to do so for a variety of reasons, such as systemic racism, natural disasters, or a lack of recorded family history. Use as much information about your family as you have access to. You decide who is included in your family. Your family unit could include your biological relatives or your primary caregivers who have different DNA. If you're unable to or would rather not focus on a family unit, feel free to connect with whomever you define as your community for the following exercises.

Create a Legacy Timeline

Do you know your family's legacy? Use your creativity to express your family or community's historical timeline. Your timeline might look like a tree with branches or a flow chart. Mark generational traumas on your timeline with red ink and generational gifts in blue ink. Take some time to learn about your family or community members. Note significant events and details about your ancestors—both negative and positive.

Write a journal entry on your observations and reflections.

> ➤ What behaviors and incidents have persisted the most in your heritage?
>
> ➤ What cycles would you like to break or repeat?
>
> ➤ How have these events, circumstances, and characteristics impacted your family dynamics and personal journey?

Consider including future events to your timeline of what you intend to accomplish. Cycle-breaking is just as much about connecting with your future as it is about understanding your past.

Start the Conversation

At times we need to be the change we are waiting to see. One way to mobilize change in your family or community is by initiating necessary dialogues that promote healing. For instance, you could organize a family meeting and encourage family members to express their thoughts and feelings about a topic.

If holding space for open dialogue will likely turn into a war zone, invite a neutral third party to mediate or host a smaller gathering of people who generally get along. The goal is to normalize conversations about sensitive topics and healthy conflict resolution. If this is not possible for your family, lean into support groups to gift yourself an emotionally safe environment that values compassionate communication.

Take a Personal Inventory

Spend some time strengthening the relationship you have with yourself. For instance, gather pictures of yourself at different ages. What relationships, thoughts, and hobbies did you have at that time? What character traits and behaviors did you inherit from your ancestors and exhibit?

Take a moment to identify which qualities you would like to nurture and which ones you'd like to disinherit going into your next life chapter. Use this information as a catalyst for next steps on your cycle-breaking journey.

Make New Traditions

I celebrated my quinceañera back in 2006. I always thought I would have one because it's traditional for many Latin American people. The reasoning behind the ceremony is to mark a fifteen-year-old's passage into womanhood. It celebrates her purity and readiness for marriage. I was far from a woman when I paraded around in my quinceañera dress as a sophomore in high school—both legally and emotionally. I certainly was not ready for marriage and I didn't feel pure as a survivor of childhood sexual abuse. Yet there I was on a sunny day in Los Angeles announcing my womanhood.

What family or cultural traditions do you participate in despite disagreeing with its meaning or being unaware of its origin? Part of healing is releasing what's in your life that doesn't align with your values or joy.

For example, I would explain to my future daughter what a quinceañera symbolizes and how it is outdated. I will then respect her decision whether to have a quinceañera or start a new family tradition.

Absent extreme circumstances, each of us has the agency to start a tradition. This could be anything from volunteering in honor of someone to creating a family holiday.

What matters is that the new tradition aligns with the legacy you'd like to create. Mark down on your calendar a new tradition you will participate in and journal about what this tradition means to you.

Break the Cycle

An architect follows a blueprint for their construction project. A tattoo artist follows a stencil. A cycle breaker follows a personal growth plan. Take time to intentionally create a timeline that outlines milestones, tools, a support system, challenges, and goals that you want to accomplish on your journey. I suggest creating this plan with a mental health professional or support group. Commit to this plan, regularly review it, recruit an accountability partner, and adjust it as you need to.

PART 4
LIMIT ACCESS TO YOU

᠎ꙮ᠎

My Pain

"I don't see a future with you, because I don't trust you." It took every ounce of courage inside me to speak these words. I said this to my ex-boyfriend only a few days after he declared his plans to marry me to my parents. The timing may seem abrupt, and trust me, it felt abrupt even to me. But this breakup was long overdue. I held on to the love I thought we had until I couldn't possibly hold on any longer. I'll refer to him as Mark.*

Our relationship lasted two and a half years but was packed with enough pain for me to need double that time to heal post-breakup. I left that relationship vowing to never be someone's rehabilitation center again. I met him when I was stressed, not in touch with myself, and hauling a suitcase overstuffed with unresolved trauma and shame. I learned the hard way that you cannot do the healing work for someone else and that a true apology is changed behavior, not empty promises.

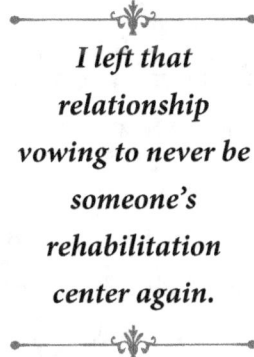

I left that relationship vowing to never be someone's rehabilitation center again.

That relationship was a poison I drank to quench my thirst for love and pain relief. I might as well have walked around with a sign that said, "Emotionally vulnerable prey." My ex-boyfriend and I mirrored one another in many ways. We carried unresolved traumas on our backs and hid dysfunctional behaviors behind a mask of achievement. Our bond formed out of shared pain and a propensity for self-sabotage. Throughout that two-and-a-half-year relationship, I played the familiar role of caretaker. I sacrificed my peace and mental health to save a relationship that was beyond saving all while struggling with an eating disorder.

We tried so hard to build a future together that we overlooked how much our pasts were replaying in the present. We deepened each other's pain and added traumas to our life stories. I take accountability for my role in my suffering and his. I am not proud of some of my words and actions during that relationship. I was an "imperfect victim." I retaliated and defended myself the best way I knew how: with my words. My "reactive abuse" was just that. I was reacting to my abuser's violence. Reactive abuse is a misnomer because it is a form of self-defense, not mutual abuse.[19] He raped me about eight months into our relationship. His sexual assault profoundly changed who I was as a person and as a girlfriend.

This relationship was a continuation of the cycle of setting myself on fire to keep someone else warm. I poured everything I had into this relationship. I intertwined my identity and worth with him. I allowed someone to make me feel low about myself on many levels. I turned to him and therapists to validate my pain so much so that I was unable to accept and understand that I was raped until after I exited the relationship.

As someone diagnosed with borderline personality disorder, relationships didn't come easy to me, let alone my first love. Our dynamic became increasingly draining. Toward the end of our relationship, I was very disconnected from my feelings. I cried for hours in the days leading up to me breaking up with him and I didn't know why I was crying. It's a scary feeling to be sobbing and genuinely have no idea why. I had to figure out and sort my feelings like a 500-piece puzzle. I desperately wanted to find a solution to our deteriorating relationship. I frantically searched for evidence of the trust I did not have in him. I neglected my own needs and dreams holding onto the dream I was sold.

Eventually, I found the courage to call a ceasefire in this warfare. I no longer wanted to fill the martyr role to enhance someone else's life. I learned many lessons from this relationship, including that I

---

[19] Alex Bachert, "What Is Reactive Abuse?" Charlie Health, July 3, 2024, https://www.charliehealth.com/post/what-is-reactive-abuse.

no longer could ignore the person in my life who needed the most care—Priscilla María. I vowed to never accept the red flags I did in this relationship again. I left this relationship and started a new one immediately with myself. I also identified who I could lean on during what I knew would be a debilitating healing process.

Social connection, which includes emotional and physical support, is key to our survival and wellness. According to the Centers for Disease Control and Prevention (CDC), people with fulfilling relationships are more likely to make decisions that improve their mental and physical health.[20] High-quality relationships can help reduce the risk of several chronic health conditions like heart disease, dementia, and depression. For instance, a car ride to a doctor's appointment or having a friend to celebrate accomplishments can go a long way. I am forever thankful to my parents, brother, and fur babies, Chules and Nanas, for being my soft landing when I free-falled from that relationship.

Letting Go of Loyalty and "Ride or Die" Culture

After her two failed marriages, my great-grandfather asked my paternal grandmother to promise him that she would never get involved with a man again. She gave and kept her word. I thought this was a daughter being loyal to her father. After that same grandmother disowned my father for choosing my mother over the family unit, my uncles didn't speak to my father either. I thought that was an example of sons being loyal to their mother. I

---

[20] "Social Connection," CDC, May 15, 2024, https://www.cdc.gov/social-connectedness/about/.

stayed with my boyfriend despite him raping me and lying consistently to me. I thought I was being loyal to the life we promised one another.

With healing and mental health treatment, I have learned to discern loyalty and true love from abuse, codependency, trauma bonding, and crossing boundaries. Loyalty is about non-judgmental support, reliability, and consistency. Love is gentle, respectful, and safe. Loyalty doesn't cost you your peace, safety, or self-esteem. Love shouldn't hurt.

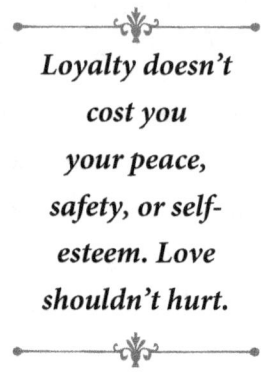

Loyalty doesn't cost you your peace, safety, or self-esteem. Love shouldn't hurt.

Ride-or-die culture is glamorized in many Latin communities. From our songs to our telenovelas to our family members, many of us were programmed to be unconditionally loyal. I've seen people in my family stay in dysfunctional marriages out of loyalty to the family unit and status quo. My culture combined with my Catholic upbringing led me to believe that self-sacrifice is the highest form of love. A ride-or-die mindset has by design a high likelihood of you "dying." Would you get on a roller coaster with a 50 percent chance of falling to the ground? Would you eat a dish with a 50 percent chance of lethal poisioning? Those are not the odds I want to take anymore.

Similar to *marianismo*, a ride-or-die dynamic demands self-sacrifice that goes beyond being reliable and generous. It means being in situations that are not good for your spirit. It means putting someone else's needs before your own. It means sacrificing your health and sanity in the name of off-brand loyalty. I have collected enough data over the years to know that a ride-or-die relationship is too costly.

Anything that costs my peace, health, and dignity is too expensive. Everyone would be held to a standard of mutual respect and support—elders, family members, and partners.

Loyalty is a core value in my family. I still hold this value close to me but I've learned to filter out the codependency and lack of boundaries. I have learned to be loyal to myself before anyone else. Specifically, I am loyal to my self-care, well-being, and happiness. I check in with myself regularly. A question I ask myself before making a decision might sound like, *Am I saying "no" to myself by saying "yes" to someone else?* If your peace or mental health is on the line, it's an uneven exchange.

Watering my relationship with myself has been the foundation for my relationship with others. Setting boundaries with myself and how I treated myself directly correlated with the health of my

Watering my relationship with myself has been the foundation for my relationship with others.

relationships. My propensity for self-harm was matched by volatile connections with others. A more grounded relationship with myself is matched by pleasant and nurturing connections. I learned that setting boundaries and raising the bar on who has access to me did not make me a callous person. Instead, it made me more in alignment with my values of compassion and self-worth by including myself.

Before my journey of healthiness, even when I was alone I would not be with myself. I distracted myself and abandoned myself through self-destructive behaviors. Hurting myself was no less unethical than hurting another person. I deserve love and safety like anyone else. I learned the difference between being lonely and alone. I have expended so much energy in some relationships, only to still feel lonely in their company. I no longer wished to feel lonely, so I reflected and discerned which connections felt one-sided or otherwise unfulfilling. Surprisingly, these unilateral connections included some of my closest romantic and platonic relationships. I realized that the state of my relationships was not only about the other person. I had to get to know the parts, and sometimes forgive the parts of myself that accepted those relationships. For instance, the fear of causing someone to feel abandoned in a way that I have felt led me to hold onto imbalanced friendships.

Setting Boundaries with Loved Ones

I recently saw a social media post that advised parents to not pressure their kids to kiss or hug people. *What a simple yet groundbreaking position to take.* I did not know I had a choice to decline interacting with my elders as a child. I can still feel the distress of hugging my grandfather who molested me. Growing up, you have to *saludar* (greet), otherwise you are *malcriado* (a bastard) and lack *educación* (manners). Reputation often came before individual safety. It was confusing to hug some relatives who tore apart my appearance, spoke poorly about my parents, or expressed racist views. I was a kid who didn't know she could say no to hugs. I then grew into an adult who didn't know how to set healthy boundaries.

Eventually, I learned that boundaries are an act of self-love. Boundaries are including *yourself* in the love you give to others. It's a way of saying "I value myself enough to protect my peace and ensure my emotional and physical safety." Boundaries are anchors that keep you grounded when the lines around you are blurred by cultural obligations, gaslighting, and guilt trips. It's not about taking from anyone but giving yourself space to thrive authentically. Boundaries are not about kicking people out of your life (although they can be) but giving them special instructions for how to remain in your life.

> *The ones who oppose your boundaries are often the ones who gain from you not having any.*

Boundaries can illuminate a course of action amidst chaos. Pay attention to who honors your boundaries and who resists. The ones who oppose your boundaries are often the ones who gain from you not having any. Takers take as long as a giver gives. Any change in dynamics often originates with the giver, particularly after they feel drained and undervalued by the taker. A helpful tip for setting boundaries is using "I" statements like "I value personal space so I'd like to spend the holidays at my home this year," or "I value respectful communication and only engage in conversations that don't include personal attacks." These statements can reduce defensiveness and foster collaboration.

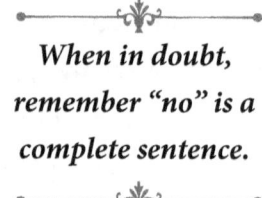

When in doubt, remember "no" is a complete sentence.

Al-Anon, an organization that supports those affected by a loved one's alcohol use disorder, coined the acronym JADE to navigate boundary-setting without Justifying, Arguing, Denying, or Explaining to the other person. When in doubt, remember "no" is a complete sentence. You do not need anyone to co-sign or approve the boundaries you set to protect your peace, safety, and happiness. Think of who you love the most.

Would you be okay with someone disrespecting or taking advantage of that person or pet? You might physically intervene or take other measures to protect your most loved being. Boundaries have the same energy for yourself.

Setting boundaries with family members has not been a smooth process, but the peace has been worth it. I had to set limits because my patience and compassion are not limitless.

Family gatherings are in theory a time of mutual love and joy, but may not be that way in practice. The holidays, for instance, are stressful for many people because of family dysfunction. This is your sign to reflect on your family dynamics and decide who you want to spend the holidays with or interact with generally.

Set Boundaries Unapologetically

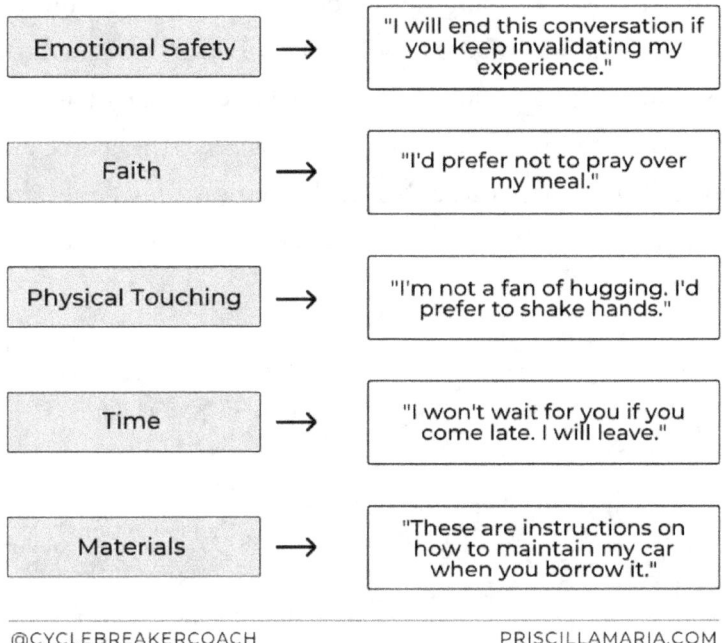

Emotional Safety	→	"I will end this conversation if you keep invalidating my experience."
Faith	→	"I'd prefer not to pray over my meal."
Physical Touching	→	"I'm not a fan of hugging. I'd prefer to shake hands."
Time	→	"I won't wait for you if you come late. I will leave."
Materials	→	"These are instructions on how to maintain my car when you borrow it."

@CYCLEBREAKERCOACH   PRISCILLAMARIA.COM

I had to hold myself accountable for the fact that I made a "family exception" to my boundaries. This clause I made for people related to me looked like not standing up for myself, forcing myself to interact with people I didn't want to, and tolerating behaviors that I would not otherwise. I slowly started to include family members in my boundary-setting. It took me so much courage to write a letter to an elder who had wounded my body image for years as well as threatened to hit me. I wrote the letter in Spanish and addressed them respectfully but honestly. I expressed my pain and gave examples of their harmful actions.

My elder responded by ripping up my letter and accused me of "hating her." Other relatives commented that "I need to let it go" and that I was "attacking her." The same people making these comments had been abused by her. I refused to backtrack from holding my elder accountable. Guess what eventually happened? She got on a call with me and she apologized. It was a beautiful moment. I also told her I was bisexual and she accepted me. I made sure to include this information for a relative who was not allowed to be openly queer.

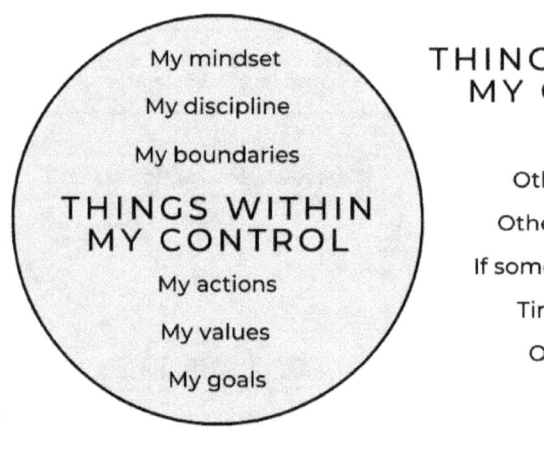

THINGS WITHIN MY CONTROL
- My mindset
- My discipline
- My boundaries
- My actions
- My values
- My goals

THINGS OUTSIDE MY CONTROL
- The past
- Others' reactions
- Other's perceptions
- If someone forgives me
- Time passing by
- Others' health
- The future

Sometimes family members with the most bark have the least bite. Sometimes family members will choose to not have a relationship with you. Also, sometimes family members you think will be least receptive are the fastest learners. Sometimes family members who adhere most to tradition ask you for advice on setting boundaries. How your family members react to your boundaries is not only outside of your control, but less important than the fact that you honored your wants and needs. Not everyone is going to be excited about you setting boundaries. Do it anyway. Do it without apologizing. Do it without explaining. Do it without negotiating. Do it however feels authentic and healing to you. Keep setting and maintaining boundaries. Your joy is worth it.

Reinventing Family Dynamics

My brother Iván is named after our father, Iván, and our father is named after our grandfather, Iván. Several other male family members carry the Iván namesake. One might assume my grandfather was a pillar of our family for so many baby boys to be named after him. Unfortunately, that was not the truth. I held resentment toward my late grandfather for many years. I was hurt that my grandfather did not raise my father or uncles. I judged him for abusing my grandmother and creating broken homes with other women. There is a certain flavor of powerlessness that you taste when you learn about your parents' traumas.

My father endured so much trauma as a boy that he says he did not experience adolescence. He was a child and then he was forced to be a man. He came close to losing his life a few times from a catastrophic 1972 earthquake to being shot at during the *Revolución Nicaragüense*. Who else could I get mad at? Nameless guerillas who were likely boys and young men without a choice? Mother Nature for the earthquake that displaced my family? My grandfather was the most visible and tangible target for the anger I felt over being powerless to change what my father suffered as a child.

My father and uncles understandably carried deep resentment toward my grandfather for a long time. My father did not have an interest in having a relationship with his father until my brother was born. I'm not encouraging anyone to forgive or reconnect with anyone who has caused them pain. I use my father as an example of how family dynamics can change and how forgiveness is a self-liberating act. My father did not forgive my grandfather for my grandfather's sake. And, believe me, my grandfather felt very entitled to forgiveness because the Bible teaches believers to honor their parents.

My father released *himself* from a prison of pain by forgiving my grandfather. He knew he could not be the father he hoped to be with anger in his heart. He forgave his father for the sake of his own inner child and two children (me and my brother). Forgiving my grandfather was a balancing act for my father because he risked being disowned by my grandmother and uncles, again. For example, he knew not to sponsor my grandfather's American citizenship despite wanting to help his father become a citizen. Never one to let others dictate his future, my father nurtured his relationship with his father over the years. Even I would criticize my father for wanting to rebuild his relationship with my grandfather. After all, where was he when my father was wearing torn pants to school, carrying books in a plastic grocery bag or surviving on government assistance? Where was he when my father graduated high school, college, law school, or business school?

My grandfather was well off but did not offer financial support to my father, uncles, and grandmother as they struggled to make ends meet. Instead, my eldest uncle took the father role and went to work with my grandmother. They lived in fear of deportation for a while as they worked in factories and housekeeping. My father explained several times that the anger I felt toward my grandfather was not my burden to carry. As fearless and intense as my father is, the inner *niño* within him would come out when it came to his father. All he ever wanted was his parents' love, but divorce, undiagnosed mental health conditions, war, poverty, and abuse complicated this for him.

I admire my father for teaching me that you can change the narrative. My father had been abused verbally and physically growing up. He had been called ugly and told he would end up just like his father.

He decided to give his kids—my brother and me—the father he never had. Of course, his parenting wasn't perfect, but he did a damn good job. He vowed not to be promiscuous, beat his wife, act selfishly, or be an absent father. He kept his promise.

As Mark Wolynn explored in *It Didn't Start with You*, generational traumas and experiences can be transmitted down the family line. For example, he discusses how the in-utero environment is so influential on someone's development because theoretically a grandmother, mother, and granddaughter occupy the same "biological environment" at one point.[21] I immediately thought of my mother when I read this. As previously mentioned, my maternal abuelita lost her son when he was fifteen years old in a mechanic accident. She was pregnant with my mother at the time.

My abuelita's body was full of grief, unimaginable pain, and cortisol while my mother was growing inside of her. My grandmother did not have access to the resources and support she needed to cope with the death of yet another one of her children. My mother's story is hers to tell, but I will say that I have zero doubt my mother was profoundly affected by untreated in-utero trauma.

My feelings toward my relatives have fluctuated over time. At times I felt anger, resentment, confusion, while other times I felt gratitude, joy, and love. Healing has allowed me to honor conflicting feelings simultaneously. I can feel disappointed by *and* incredibly thankful for my Abuelita Bertha's decisions. I applaud her for choosing to radically change family dynamics. She came from a Catholic background and had borne seven children with my grandfather. Culture, religion, and family dictated she stick beside her husband. From what I've been told, she consulted with a local priest who gave his blessing for my grandmother to do what she ultimately did.

My Abuelita Bertha told my mother and aunt that they would be going on vacation to Los Angeles to visit family members that already immigrated. My grandfather and everybody else were also

---

[21] Wolynn, *It Didn't Start with You*, 25.

told that they were going on vacation. My mother said, "I came on a Friday for vacation and was enrolled in school by Monday." I often wonder what was the breaking point for my abuelita because she had known about his pedophilia for years. I have my theories but I don't know for sure.

As I write these words, I risk further backlash from some of my relatives. That's okay because my intentions are pure. I write this for my relatives' inner children who didn't have a voice or an understanding of what was happening to them, including my mother's inner niña. I do this for my future children so that they know what history not to repeat. I do this so that their mother is untethered to repetitive, unhealthy cycles when she meets them. I do this for every person reading this on their healing journey. To show that it's possible to build a new civilization from the ruins of another.

> *Whatever was done to you or in your family's past does not have to live in your present or future.*

Two things can be true at once: Your family members could have tried their best to care for you and also caused you harm. Whatever was done to you or in your family's past does not have to live in your present or future. Breaking cycles to create a new family legacy is possible. It takes learning and unlearning, listening to the said and unsaid, speaking courageously when you feel the most vulnerable, and continuing forward when others might try to pull you backward. How others react to the chapters in your healing story is outside of your control. Not everyone deserves to meet the healed version of yourself.

Raising the Bar in Relationships and Lifestyle Choices

"I'm facing fifteen years in prison."

My heart sank when I heard this. I hadn't been dating Marquise* that long but long enough to care about his well-being, for him to meet friends and family, and to feel distraught. Ultimately, he did not serve that much time. I don't recall the specifics of his case but I do remember running into him at a club about a year later. I was undiagnosed with borderline personality disorder in college. I didn't know what I know now about how people living with BPD often move quickly and intensely in their romantic relationships or that trauma bonding does not equal compatibility. Trauma bonding was what glued me to Marquise. His father struggled with addiction and my brother had just entered rehab. I felt like he could understand my pain at a time when my brother's addiction was kept secret from most people. A symptom of BPD is a fear of abandonment. I felt abandoned by my brother, and Marquise's pending legal case pushed me over the edge. I believed I was suddenly losing another person I cared about. I ended up going to see an on-campus counselor because I could not concentrate in class.

My experience with Marquise was not an isolated event. I gravitated toward people who were hurting and had dysfunctional backgrounds romantically and platonically. Part of me wanted to

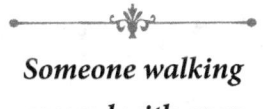

Someone walking around with open wounds is liable to bleed all over someone who didn't cut them.

help and fix them. Part of me lived vicariously through them. Part of me wanted to give them the level of support that I secretly wanted. Someone walking around with open wounds is liable to bleed all over someone who didn't cut them. I learned the hard way over the years to be selective with who I allow into my space.

Raising the bar on who has access to you is not about being bougie or smug. Limiting access to you is about being intentional about who you share your energy with and whose energy you consume. Avoid people who just want to get something out of you, don't respect your values, or don't nurture your growth and instead surround yourself with people that enhance your life and encourage you in the best ways. From a scale of an "everybody free before 11 p.m." night club to the White House, how exclusive are you?

There are over eight billion people in the world. We do not have to limit ourselves to our hometown or to people we share DNA with. We can curate our chosen family. I used to think friendships were forever. I've learned that you can feel deeply connected to someone one year and speak seldom the next year without bad blood. It's okay for relationships to

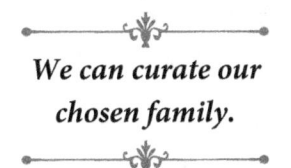

We can curate our chosen family.

evolve. Sometimes the version of yourself that attracted and accepted a friendship is no longer who you are today. I also learned that how someone treats me is not a reflection of my worth. *I know* I am worthy regardless if someone thinks I am an angel or a demon.

I don't know much about sports. I couldn't tell you LeBron James's career highlights, what training it took for him to earn all of his accolades, or even the logistics of a basketball game. If, for whatever reason, I am given a LeBron James jersey, I would look into selling it. I would see what I could get out of the jersey and move on. A zealous fan of James, on the other hand, might frame the jersey, post about it all over social media, and hold onto it with joy and respect for James's accomplishments. This fan would know the value of preserving the jersey and all the grit, hard work, and talent the jersey represents. The jersey would be much more than a money grab for this fan. Same jersey but different perceptions of value. Choose people who value you beyond what they can profit off of you.

Your professional relationships also matter to your wellness. Take a moment and reflect on your work connections. What boundaries do you have in the workplace? Do you feel safe, valued, and trusted by your employer? High School Priscilla and College Priscilla became Employed Priscilla who similarly struggled to advocate for herself. Like in school, I overextended myself, overachieved, and viewed my supervisors like all-knowing authority figures. For example, I was asked to shred paper during a college internship at a legal office in Baltimore. I did not question my supervisor and spent a significant time in a separate room shredding stacks of paper.

I naively thought I was shredding confidential paper that urgently needed to be discarded. It wasn't until an employee told me in confidence that shredding paper wasn't a good use of my time or skill set that it finally hit me. I was put aside to do "busy work."

This situation reminded me of an internship I did during high school at a nonprofit. One of my internship supervisors asked me when I would start at the local community college. I said I was going to Johns Hopkins University in the fall. He looked at me in disbelief. I felt discouraged by having my efforts overlooked and my abilities predetermined instead of truly recognized. Seeking mentorship from Latina professionals as an adult helped boost my self-esteem. They understood the cultural expectations to play small and simply be grateful, and instead encouraged me to amplify my voice and potential. Surrounding yourself with supportive people can make a big difference on motivation, opportunities, and quality of life. I would have continued shrinking and doubting myself had I bought into the limitations set by those internship supervisors. Instead, I curate a community full of people like my Latina mentors who remind me of my worth and help me see possibilities not limits.

More influential to your wellness than a mentor or supervisor is what you put into, onto, and around your body. The relationship you have with yourself as reflected in your lifestyle choices is essential to assess. Many conversations about nourishment center on what we eat but consumption goes beyond food. What we consume energetically affects our mindset and mental and physical health. Consider your social media feed. Whose content are you regularly digesting? What type of content are you consistently consuming? I noticed that my nervous system feels much lighter when I watch cute videos of puppies on social media than when I watch news clips. Your body will tell you what it needs more of and less of.

The drugs, if any, you consume can have a significant impact on your mind and body. Researchers have found that drugs like cannabis, ketamine, and MDMA can be used in psychiatry. I am not a "drugs are bad" proponent. I am a proponent of education and people making informed decisions. I share openly about my past relationship with alcohol to bring awareness to its effects. Alcohol was a crutch for me and it took me years to accept that crutches are used when something is broken. My spirit was fractured and needed healing. I could no longer justify blacking out and binge drinking a known carcinogen. Letting go of alcohol allowed me to let go of people and habits that Drunk Priscilla mistakenly thought were good for her.

Alcohol was a crutch for me and it took me years to accept that crutches are used when something is broken.

Studies have shown that a plant can react positively or negatively to the vibrations of our words.[22] If a plant is affected by negative energy, how much do you think your soul is affected by negative people, habits, and media? Surround yourself with people who

---

[22] Seetha Dodd, "'They respond to vibrations': does talking to plants actually help them grow?" *The Guardian*, January 10, 2021, https://www.theguardian.com/lifeandstyle/2021/jan/11/they-respond-to-vibrations-does-talking-to-plants-actually-help-them-grow.

replenish you, encourage your dreams, respect your boundaries, and care about your fulfilment.

Finding Support

I went to mostly predominantly-white schools growing up. Toni Morrison once said, "If there's a book that you want to read, but it hasn't been written yet, then you must write it."[23] I channeled this energy in the fourth high school I attended by founding a student club. I created the Tolerance Club my senior year to provide a safe space for global majority people and allies to meet and discuss ways to foster belonging in our predominantly-white high school. I founded the Cycle Breakers Club, LLC in 2022 with the same spirit to provide life coaching for cycle breakers. I wanted to offer the support I needed when I was younger and didn't experience.

Have you noticed the more you hang out with someone the more you adopt parts of them? You might start using some of the slang they use, listening to the music they introduced you to, or replicating parts of their style. If you surround yourself with doomsdayers, you are going to be more likely to view the world with pessimism and distrust. If you surround yourself with vegans, you are going to be more likely to value the ethical treatment of animals.

We are not meant to live in solitary confinement, literally or metaphorically. Human connection is a human right as much as it is a human need. Connection can fill a void the way drugs could

---

[23] Spoken at Toni Morrison's 1981 speech to the Ohio Arts Council.

never. Loving connection can bandage the deepest wounds the way isolation and self-sabotage could never. I encourage you to discover your community virtually, in person, or both and tap into collective strength, wisdom, and resources. Community-building is an ongoing process that opens you up to opportunity. Your community will likely evolve as you do and that's okay.

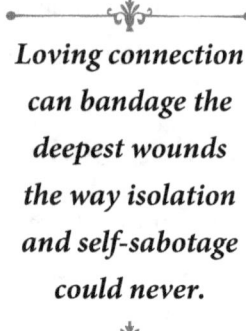

Loving connection can bandage the deepest wounds the way isolation and self-sabotage could never.

Being in support groups is an opportunity to stock up your mental health toolkit with new strategies, modalities, and resources. The Sober Black Girls Club is an example of a supportive and empowering space. This was the first recovery space I've been in centered on Black women and nonbinary people. I had the honor of co-hosting Tuesday night meetings for queer BIPOC folks. It was the first support group I'd been a part of that didn't revolve around white experiences. I felt safety and comfort being in community with people who could understand my experiences on a deep level. A sense of belonging can be a saving grace.

Empowering Stories of Transformation

Readiness is a decision and not a feeling, in my experience. Waiting for the "right time" often means convenience or waiting for the nerves to go away. I've met some incredible people on my healing journey who reinforce that happiness and transformation do not just happen to you. They are products of perseverance, consistency, and choosing growth over comfort.

I've included parts of their stories below for inspiration and guidance. Their testimonies show what's possible when we get out of our own way.

Iván X.

Lay down and close your eyes for ten seconds then open them. Now, imagine before you closed your eyes you could run track and play tennis. But after you open your eyes you can't lift a fork. You can't spell your name. You can't move your legs. You have no idea how, what, where, when, or why. That's how my brother experienced his roughly six-month coma. One moment he was walking and driving around wherever he wanted to and the next he was on a hospital bed needing around-the-clock care. He survived his traumatic brain injury against all odds.

Medical practitioners placed limits on him over the years. Iván would have never emerged from his hospital bed—let alone find a job, finish his college degree, or take steps—had he accepted limitations placed on him. He accomplished all those "impossible" goals and more because he chose to believe in his ability the most. We as a family understood that doctors provide their best professional advice but also that each traumatic brain injury is unique. We put faith in God and Iván's efforts. Iván's growth mindset catapulted him to reach gains beyond what any medical practitioner predicted and he has not given up to this day. Iván continues on his journey to walk and live independently. He remains sober and focused on healing and growth.

Kaaliyah*

Kaaliyah is one of my first paying coaching clients. We work together to this day. She is a testament to what is possible when you approach life with open-mindedness, courage, and tenacity. She was trapped in an abusive marriage, a cycle of binge drinking, and a monotonous lifestyle when we started coaching. We created a road map for her transformation that included defining boundaries, discrediting self-limiting beliefs, and pursuing goals outside her safe space.

Today, Kaaliyah lives and travels independently for the first time in her life. She filed for divorce from her abuser, moved to a new city, replaced drinking with self-care routines, and set firm boundaries in her personal and professional relationships. This evolution cost Kaaliyah her old life, behaviors, and thought patterns. She had to challenge a lifetime's worth of cultural expectations, negative self-talk, and generational curses. It is an honor to witness Kaaliyah replace hopelessness with self-empowerment.

Support Groups

Humans are social creatures by design. Ample research confirms that we need social interaction to not only thrive but to survive. Social connection can improve your physical health, happiness, and lifespan.[24] Think about how much time you spend interacting

---

[24] "Connect with Others," Mental Health America, https://mhanational.org/resources/connect-with-others/, accessed July 14, 2025.

with another person virtually or in person. Have you ever felt the soothing warmth of someone's embrace during a challenging time? How often do you high-five or dap up a friend to celebrate a win? When was the last time you shared your thoughts on social media for others to read?

As the Swedish proverb goes, "Shared joy is a double joy; shared sorrow is half sorrow." This statement captures the essence of a support group. These groups are opportunities to witness and participate in courageous action. Many

"Shared joy is a double joy; shared sorrow is half sorrow."

people grew up in homes where it was not emotionally safe to be vulnerable and expressive. Support groups are opportunities to experience emotional safety, empowerment, accountability, and motivation. Not every support group, however, is built the same. I have seen different cultural and gender identities express their deepest fears, regrets, and wounds within the same space. I have also had to remove people from support groups. My recommendation is to search for support groups that value trauma-informed practices and have clear boundaries and policies. A support group you are compatible with and feel supported by could be very helpful on your healing journey.

Sociologist Brené Brown said, "Vulnerability begets vulnerability."[25] I've witnessed this phenomenon firsthand on countless occasions

---

[25] Brené Brown, *Daring Greatly: How the Courage to Be Vulnerable Transforms the Way We Live, Love, Parent, and Lead* (Penguin, 2012), 54.

while facilitating hundreds of support groups and listening to thousands of shares. Vulnerability begetting vulnerability in childhood might look like going down a steep water slide after seeing your friend go beforehand. It might look like asking someone to dance after seeing your friend ask someone in adolescence. It might look like allowing your tears to fall after seeing someone courageously share their feelings in adulthood.

Mental health conditions like alcohol use disorder, more commonly known as alcoholism, are often stigmatized. I've heard numerous people describe the judgment, rejection, and ridicule they have faced due to their mental health challenges. A support group is a chance to be surrounded by people on a similar path and feel less alone. I have witnessed people enter a support group with wounded self-esteem and gradually shed self-limiting beliefs to emerge more confident and self-compassionate after consistently attending support group meetings. For many, community is the antidote for the poison eroding their soul.

Immersing yourself around people who "get it" can strengthen your confidence and conviction in your decisions. Most of the support groups I facilitated have been for people recovering from alcohol use disorder. Many participants had been convicted of DUIs, lost their jobs, severed relationships, and lived with an unbearable amount of shame. Three days of sobriety may not seem like a big deal to someone who does not have an alcohol dependency. Those who are also fighting for their sobriety know how incredible and difficult seventy-two hours of sobriety is. Like vulnerability, resilience can be contagious. With time, many people disclosed traumas they had never spoken about before, described ways they stood up for themselves, opened up about leaving toxic relationships, and released raw emotions.

Below are some kind words from Cycle Breakers I coached in a group setting over the years:

Nicholas Roberts

"I state the following in the best possible way: Coach Priscilla is the only person in my adult life to bring me to tears . . . Her presence is wrapped in love, and always augmented by deep experiential knowledge and wisdom . . . She has helped me (and countless others) think in new ways about myself and my journey in health and wellness. Her talent is remarkable."

Zoe H.

"I worked with Priscilla for just over three months and it was one of the most transformative experiences in my adult life. Her nonjudgmental and supportive coaching made me feel truly seen and heard for the first time . . . Choosing to work with Priscilla has undoubtedly been the best decision I've made this year."

Miki Byrne

"Priscilla is an amazing life coach and support group facilitator. I have always felt so comfortable to speak about my demons in her presence, because I know that she has been through some demons of her own. To be able to relate to someone in such a vulnerable and personal way is deeply humbling and special. I am a survivor of sexual assault, and her Trauma Support Meeting was the first place I felt safe enough to open up about my story on an online platform . . ."

Holly G.

"For nearly two years, I had the privilege of attending Priscilla's online community meetings, which consistently attracted over a hundred participants. Her calming presence and genuine warmth always put me at ease. Her professional, unscripted, humanistic responses, rooted in both personal experience and formal education, made me feel heard and valued . . ."

Summary and Self-Care

Recap:

> *"Heal so that you no longer accept apologies without changed behavior, the bare minimum as effort, codependency as loyalty, or trauma bonding as love."*
>
> ~ PRISCILLA MARÍA

Own Your Truth

> ➢ Share, release, process, or all of the above to whatever extent you find helpful. Your healing, your rules.
>
> ➢ Amplify your inner coach while quieting your inner hater to harness your inner strength.
>
> ➢ Become fluent in authentic self-expression regardless of public opinion.

> ➤ Embrace what is beyond your comfort zone by building your emotional endurance of rejection and invalidation from others.

Set Boundaries on Your Terms

> ➤ Liberate yourself from any toxic behaviors and dynamics that require you to sacrifice your peace, safety, or authenticity.

> ➤ Empower yourself to set and maintain personal and professional boundaries.

> ➤ Define loyalty in a way that protects your mental and physical wellness.

> ➤ Pursue goals, relationships, and experiences that align with your values and joy.

Choose Your Company Wisely

> ➤ Examine present family dynamics and decide how you would like to maintain or change them.

> ➤ Absorb and implement strategies for boundaries from resources like *Boundaries* by Henry Cloud and Dr. Townsend.

> ➤ Assess which relationships you would like to nurture and which ones you'd like to outgrow to strengthen your support network.

> ➤ Immerse yourself in environments, such as support groups, that promote growth, reciprocity, compassion, and authenticity.

Cycle Breaker Challenge: Practice Makes Progress

Practice Mindfulness

Mindfulness is an intentional practice needed now more than ever in an era of constant social media notifications, omnipresent advertisements, and breaking news headlines. The practice requires us to be in the moment without judgment. I gently challenge you to implement mindful communication in your social interactions for a week by "practicing the pause." During virtual and in-person conversations, take a deep breath and a moment to carefully craft your responses. This mindful moment can be as long as you need it to be to make a decision Future You will be proud of. This exercise could help you communicate your needs, set boundaries, and make less knee-jerk decisions in your relationships. Opportunities to practice mindfulness include eating and walking mindfully.

Practice Self-Care

Reflect on your schedule from the last three days. What percentage of your time did you dedicate to practicing self-care? Do you think this is an adequate amount based on how you are feeling today? They say we make time for what's important to us. What do your answers say about how important self-care is to you?

I recommend carving at least fifteen minutes of your day for the next thirty days for a self-care activity that allows you to recharge, reduce stress, and cater to yourself. Some self-care ideas include stretching, nutritious food, and spending time in nature. Take note of your stress levels, sleep patterns, and moods at the beginning and end of the thirty days. What do you think you will notice? Use your responses to create a long-term self-care plan.

Practice Boundaries

Setting and maintaining boundaries can be an intimidating exercise. Like an athlete preparing for an intense match or an attorney gearing up for stressful litigation, practice is key to navigating obstacles on your healing journey. I encourage you to engage in a role-play exercise with someone you trust to practice verbalizing your boundaries. Get your reps in saying "no" to circumstances that do not align with your values, comfort, or energy. Like any skill, the more you practice, the more likely you are to progress and feel confident.

Practice Connection

Limiting access to you is not about isolation but about raising the bar of who you exchange energy with. It's about feeding your soul with meaningful connections. Set aside some time to reflect on what connections you hold closest to you, what connections you'd like to reconsider or let go, and what connections you'd like to form. Opportunities to meet people include wellness activities, volunteering events, and workout classes.

PART 5
TURN TRAUMAS INTO COMMAS

———— ༄ ༄ ༄ ————

I Found My Voice

Serves *her right*, I thought as my brother, cousin, and I continued driving around.

It was a few days after my high school graduation and I recognized a classmate driving beside us. I promptly mouthed expletives and raised my middle fingers at her. She understandably became terrified and pulled off to the side of the road. I did this because she had tagged me in her Facebook picture as a "quiet, weird girl." I was in the background of her picture and had no idea I had been photographed until I happened to see the post. I wanted her to feel an ounce of hurt that I felt over the years being ostracized as "quiet," "weird," and "ugly."

I was tired of being judged for my shyness and not fitting into the predominantly-white schools I attended. I had no control when or where my father's job would take us next. But for the next four years, I knew I would be living in the same place: Baltimore, Maryland. Specifically, at Johns Hopkins University. This was the first time in my life that I knew I wouldn't be moving anywhere for years. This meant so much to me after four high schools in three different states between 2005–2007 alone. This new chapter gave me a spark of confidence, and standing up to this classmate was a step toward finding my voice and shedding my "good girl" mask. I wanted to bury the version of myself that tolerated so much disrespect in the suburbs and start anew.

I would be living in a majority Black city with students from around the world. I wouldn't be the "new girl" because everyone in the incoming freshman class would be a newcomer. I vowed to myself that I would not allow another peer to make me feel small because of my appearance, ethnicity, or introversion. For example, some students in the high schools I went to in Connecticut and Maryland openly made racist comments toward Latinos and Black people. I recall going into AP English Literature and Composition and seeing "White America" written on the board.

The journey from selective mutism to professional speaker was one full of trial and error, grit, creativity, and some uncouth behavior. Although I'm not proud of how I confronted that classmate on the road, I did the gesture as a representation of the overall shift I was beginning to make away from being obedient and playing small to standing up for myself. The irony of me being paid for the voice that lay dormant inside me for years would make Adolescent Priscilla so proud.

I had my first paid college speaking event in Tennessee at Lane College for its Minority Mental Health Summit panel in 2023. This speaking event was far more than a professional milestone. I heal a part of myself every time I speak in front of a group of people. I let the younger version of myself feel heard, included, and valued. The same girl who at times ate lunch at school alone was now being paid to express herself. I had found purpose in my pain and a way to offer a lifeline to people who might be struggling.

I had found purpose in my pain and a way to offer a lifeline to people who might be struggling.

I experienced a full-circle moment in April of 2025 when I spoke at my alma mater. Out of all locations, I was hired to speak in the same building I lived in during the height of my self-destruction in college. I was more nervous to be in the epicenter of chaotic and painful memories than to deliver my actual program. I had been in the very room I spoke at years ago as an overwhelmed student, never imagining I would one day return as a professional speaker. It was healing to have faculty and students trust my wisdom and replace a past nightmare with a dream come true.

I hold each vulnerable share before, during, and after my talks close to my heart. One person recently shared that she did not know her eating disorder had any correlation to her trauma until she heard my story, while another asked for advice on how to support her sister who lives with borderline personality disorder. Sometimes the shares are in the form of tears and hugs. I am honored to have a platform to speak about the often unspoken and normalize conversations about mental health.

I chose not to take my traumas to the grave. They had been buried long enough deep in the back of my mind. I initially chose to exhume the skeletons of my past for my healing, but with time I realized my story could facilitate someone else's healing. I knew this to be true because I had benefitted from hearing about others living with my diagnoses and surviving similar traumas. I wanted others to feel understood the way I did from hearing others' healing journeys. The thought of getting through to someone when they needed support the most helped me push through the doubt, fear of judgment, and imposter syndrome I experienced early in my speaking and coaching career.

Turning traumas into commas is up for interpretation. The concept centers on reclaiming your power after a traumatic experience and making art out of agony. It could mean pursuing a career that allows you to apply and profit from your post-traumatic growth. It could mean using your voice to impact thousands or even millions of people. It could be using your influence to raise beaucoup funding for a cause you are passionate about. Dr. Maya Angelou is a testament to what can lay on the other side of healing from trauma. Angelou stopped speaking as a child for nearly five years because she believed her testimony had led to her rapist's murder. She went on to publish more than thirty bestselling titles, receive over fifty honorary degrees, recite her poetry at a presidential inauguration, and advocate courageously alongside Malcolm X and Dr. Martin Luther King Jr. for civil rights protections. The little girl who was silenced by trauma became a voice of healing, truth-telling, and empowerment for millions.

Discover Your Superpower

I speak from firsthand experience when I say that traumatic experiences can rob someone of their sense of self, safety, and belonging. I have let people destroy my peace because they couldn't find their own. I accepted apologies without improved behavior. I gravitated toward chaos in the external world that matched my chaotic internal world.

I'm here to remind every trauma survivor of what I wish I learned in my twenties. We each have at least one superpower within us. Your superpower is not necessarily a talent, profitable skill set, or supernatural ability. It's what makes up the core of you and adds exceptional value to your life and others' lives. Examples of super-powers include deep empathy, powerful intuition, and effective

We each have at least one superpower within us.

communication. Finding your superpower involves self-curiosity and discovery of your genuine self.

Discovering your true self is an ongoing process that involves breaking free from trauma, self-limiting beliefs, and social pressures. It's okay if you do not have everything figured out as you read this. Clarity and confidence in your future will come with consistent action. This process takes courage because it's often easier to blend in than to stand out. I decided that blending in cost too much—my peace of mind, truth, and joy. I spent one year too many hiding parts of myself, contorting myself to fit into boxes crafted by society, and people-pleasing those closest to me. I chose the temporary discomfort of stepping outside my comfort zone over a lifetime of feeling uncomfortable in my skin.

My strengths, weaknesses, achievements, and shortcomings make up the recipe to my superpower—authenticity. Authenticity is the key that opens doors of opportunities for me to connect and impact more people in my professional and personal life than I could have imagined. I can leverage my diverse lived experiences to meet all types of people where they are. My authenticity as a speaker and coach invites others to be vulnerable and honest.

I am able to live authentically after inviting self-compassion and evicting self-deprecation. This switch took many therapy sessions, tear-filled conversations, journal entries, and support group meetings. Gradually, I learned to accept all parts of myself, including the parts that make me cringe, sad, embarrassed, and insecure. For example, a feature of my borderline personality disorder diagnosis is my deep empathy for others, which has strengthened me as a coach and speaker. I can own and leverage my diagnosis without internalizing the stigma that some people perpetuate.

Two Things Can Be True at Once

I am humble	and	**ambitious.**
I am open-minded	and	**have boundaries.**
I am confident	and	**experience anxiety.**
I am giving	and	**put myself first.**
I am learning	and	**unlearning.**

@CYCLEBREAKERCOACH   PRISCILLAMARIA.COM

My healing journey like everyone else's is nonlinear. The fluctuations continue, but over time the intensity and frequency of my mental health flare-ups have decreased. My goal is not to experience heaven on earth but to no longer put myself through hell and call that a life. At this point in my life inauthenticity is a deal-breaker. If a relationship or situation

My goal is not to experience heaven on earth but to no longer put myself through hell and call that a life.

costs me my authenticity it is out of my budget. No one and nothing is worth abandoning myself and the commitment I made to gift myself the most fulfilling life I can.

Be Unapologetically Resilient

I wish I understood the value of mistakes earlier as a recovering perfectionist because it would have saved me negative self-talk and procrastination. According to neuroscience, our brains learn from making mistakes through a process known as "error-related negativity." Apart from learning, mistakes also help us adapt and grow because they make us more resilient. Resilience refers to an ability to recuperate from physical, mental, or emotional stress and can be influenced by such factors as genetics, environment, and social support.[26] Resilience is not about reacting less to stress but adapting more to stress.

The road to converting traumas into commas is paved with courage and perseverance. Some ways to strengthen your resilience muscle include: facing challenges with a problem-solving attitude, surrounding yourself with people who uplift your spirit, and nourishing your body and mind with energy givers like whole foods and sunlight.

Fearlessly Pursue Your Dreams

The Autobiography of Malcolm X sparked a fire inside of me when I read it at fourteen years old. I daydreamed about sharing unapologetic

---

[26] Richard G. Hunter, Jason D. Gray, and Bruce S. McEwen, "The Neuroscience of Resilience," *Journal for the Society for Social Work and Research* 9, no. 2 (Summer 2018), https://www.journals.uchicago.edu/doi/full/10.1086/697956.

thoughts in interviews, championing racial justice, becoming a civil rights attorney, and writing my autobiography as an adult. His unfiltered rhetoric inspired me to complete my freshman research project on the myth of race and the origins of racist ideology.

I stood in front of mostly white kids and told them about the very white supremacy that they benefit from. It was the most I'd ever spoken in class. I knew then my purpose was to advocate, educate, and facilitate healing.

Over time I lost sight of my dream to make Malcolm X proud. I relocated with my family often, experienced trauma, and battled mental health conditions. The storm started to clear after I graduated from law school in 2017. I courageously moved to Michigan from California in 2018 after ending a romantic relationship that turned aromantic and abusive. I left the person I planned to marry, have children with, and build a forever home with. I traded his lies for my truth, swapped chaos for a chance at peace, and boarded a plane with no itinerary for my future. My authenticity and our toxic relationship were incompatible. I *had* to leave to become the woman of my dreams.

The weight of others' criticism weighed more than my suitcase. "You better get your shit together, Priscilla. Your generation in the family hasn't done shit with their lives," said my uncle. "You are not doing what you went to school for. This is a hobby. You identify too much with your trauma," said my therapist. "It's not too late to take the bar," said many. I didn't know what I would do with my life when I boarded that plane, but I knew who I did not want to be and what I did not want to do.

It took years of trial and error, courage-building, and breaking through self-limiting beliefs to curate the career of *my* dreams. "Some type of activist-speaker-healer-writer with Malcolm X vibes" is not a search that yields results on LinkedIn or Indeed. I cast a wide net and sent out countless applications. No response was the most common response I received from employers. I was most interested in social justice jobs, but most paid too little or required experience I lacked. *What had I done wrong?* I followed the college formula marketed as a guarantee for higher earning potential and job security. I graduated from top schools with a Bachelor's and a Juris Doctor. Yet I received rejection letter after rejection letter, or worse, radio silence from employers.

I could have saved seven years of higher education, a hefty price tag, and made a higher income pursuing a vocation. *Maybe, I should just take the Bar or find a secure corporate job.* I was stuck and going in circles because I lacked confidence and direction. I was not listening to, let alone trusting, my inner voice. I was a housekey trying to unlock the wrong house. I didn't fit into what I was trying desperately to be a part of. I wasn't *meant to fit in* but I had yet to realize that. I cared too much about appeasing others and fitting into society's standards.

I allowed others' opinions to distort my self-image and weaken my self-trust. Thankfully, I listened to a faint inner voice that said, "Stop." Stop living on autopilot. Stop living your life according to others' opinions. Stop starving yourself of the love you feed others. The first step in reclaiming my life was deciding not to sit for the Bar or practice as an attorney. I didn't remotely have things figured out but I knew one thing—the life I wanted was in the discomfort and vulnerability I was avoiding.

I had the building blocks to build a comfortable life from the outside looking in, but looks are notoriously deceiving. Despite it all, I was physically, emotionally, and mentally drained. I decided to accept more and expect less. I accepted that I could never transform into the woman I am meant to become if nothing changed. I stopped expecting circumstances and people to change and accepted what was in plain sight. I learned that "yes" lives in the land of "no" and to trust that rejection is redirection, including what and who I reject.

I said "no" to living another day as a woman I no longer recognized and "yes" to a personal revolution. I chose the unknown. I chose possibility. I chose to break the cycle. The difference between your life today and the one you'd like to live could be one decision. When and how you make that decision is within your control.

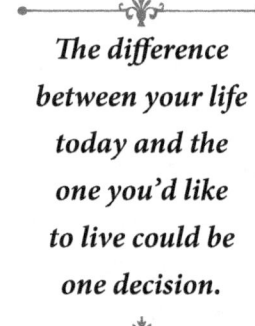

The difference between your life today and the one you'd like to live could be one decision.

Break Up with Your Inner Critic

They say a picture is worth a thousand words. Those thousand words may not tell half of your story. Pick a random selfie of you on your phone. The shape of your lips and eyebrows may give away how you're feeling inside. But a photo will not reveal your exact thoughts. Some argue that the most intimate relationship we experience is the one we have with ourselves. No one has access to our internal dialogue unless we let them in. Therefore, it is up to us to assess the way we speak to ourselves, the thoughts we buy into, and whether our self-limiting beliefs are pebbles, cobblestones, or boulders on our path to finding our voices.

Take a moment and reflect on the last time you made a mistake. What did your internal dialogue sound like? Now take a moment and remember the last time you accomplished something. What did your self-talk sound like then? How you speak to yourself matters the most. Your mind is always listening to what you say about yourself. Not only that, but it believes what you tell it. An "I'm so stupid" can

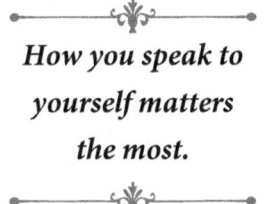

How you speak to yourself matters the most.

reverberate through your body and get stored as a self-belief. I speak from experience when I say that your body absorbs and is influenced by what you supply it. I once burned my wrist with a flat iron because of negative self-talk. Had anyone suggested it I would have looked at them like they had three heads, but when my mind told me I deserved to self-harm, I didn't question it.

It took me years to realize that the negative voice that harshly criticized my mistakes and robbed me of grace did not belong to me. I became curious about when I first started having self-critical thoughts and connected the dots. I realized that I had adopted the voice of family members and peers over the years as mine. Unhealed trauma added credibility to these critical thoughts.

Call Out Your Inner Critic

Our minds are the ultimate echo chambers. There is no one else in this world who can hear our inner thoughts and challenge them in real time. Negative words like "I'm broken" can trigger stress hormones, whereas positive words like "I'm learning" can increase cognitive reasoning and motivation. Making simple shifts from "I have to go to work" to "I *get* to go to work" can go a long way. Saying "I'm thankful for the lessons I couldn't learn in a gentle way" versus "I'm so stupid for how I behaved when I was in pain" feels softer on the nervous system. Separating your authentic self from your inner hater is key to taking your power back.

Separating your authentic self from your inner hater is key to taking your power back.

Our thoughts are automatic, temporary, and only exist within our minds. Thoughts are not facts and only as real as we make them through our actions and choices in response to them. Consequently, it's common to accept our intrusive and negative thoughts as the truth even when they are false. For example, a person having the thought that they are worthless does not mean they are in fact without worth. Our thoughts and feelings can signal to us what we care about, what we may need to heal, or what we are experiencing, but they do not always reflect reality or objective truth.

Cycle-breaking requires breaking up with harmful thought patterns. One way to challenge ways of thinking that don't serve your joy is through the cognitive behavioral therapy technique, the "Three Cs." This strategy involves *catching, challenging,* and *changing* an unhelpful thought. Application could sound like, "I am having the thought that I am worthless. This is unrealistic, unhealthy, and unhelpful. I am one-of-a-kind, bring joy to others, and have accomplished so much. I am worthy of the same grace I give others and am enough just as I am."

It could be helpful to think of what you might say to a loved one who is having the same thought of worthlessness during the "challenge" and "change" stages. Consider keeping a journal and documenting when and how you used the Three C's. Take note of any patterns and how much progress you make in silencing your inner troll. For example, you might notice that your inner critic is louder during certain situations and around specific people. Use this data to make decisions about who and what you give your energy to.

Apart from the Three C's, try to create psychological distance from your thoughts. For instance, reframing "I am worthless" to "I am having the thought that I am worthless" could help you observe your thought without being emotionally consumed by it. Another tactic to combat negative thoughts is asking yourself, "Who said this?" Next time you have an unsettling and unsubstantiated thought like *My friend hates me*, ask yourself, "Who said that my friend hates me?" If the response is "Nobody but my mind," that is like hitting a stop sign and giving yourself the chance to pause and reassess your next move.

Amplify Your Inner Coach

Your inner cheerleader can overpower your inner critic. Putting yourself down is not morally superior to putting another person down. No one deserves to be verbally attacked, including you BY you. Your inner coach reminds you that you are not your failures or mistakes but a person worthy of grace. Your inner coach provides empathy, positivity, and encouragement that pours back into you the ambition, confidence, and self-compassion that your inner critic takes. Your inner critic breaks down your spirit and steps on your dreams, whereas an inner coach breathes hope into you and applauds your aspirations.

Your inner critic wants you to stay tethered to your trauma, pain, and doubt. Your inner coach tells you that your trauma is part of your story but does not define you. Connecting with my inner coach has allowed me to embrace my strengths, values, and ambitions.

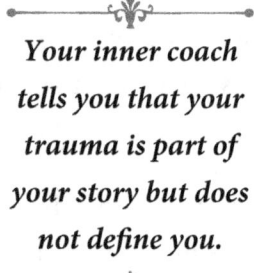

Your inner coach tells you that your trauma is part of your story but does not define you.

Ways I bond with my inner coach include reciting affirmations, maintaining a success journal of my accomplishments, and gifting myself support, self-care, and rest. Your inner coach can help heal different parts of you. Many of us did not receive the support we needed as a child. Developing a relationship with your inner coach is essential to reparenting your inner child. An inner coach validates your feelings, cultivates self-compassion, sets boundaries with yourself, and meets your needs the way a parent should.

Proceed with Patience

Reframing self-limiting beliefs and replacing negative self-talk with a growth mindset is a gradual process. With consistent effort, self-kindness, and accountability, you can rise from doubt to empowerment. Experiencing setbacks, frustration, and uncertainty are to be expected. Any obstacle is an opportunity to implement tools, refine skills, and show yourself how much you've grown. The key to this never-ending journey is to keep the momentum going *despite* the ups and downs.

A frequent hurdle on a self-growth journey is comparison. It's tempting and human to compare ourselves to others, but be aware of what purpose comparison serves you. Is comparison a reference point for inspiration? Does comparison amplify your inner critic or inner coach? My advice is if you are going to compare yourself to someone, I encourage you to compare yourself to who you were last year, six months ago, or even yesterday.

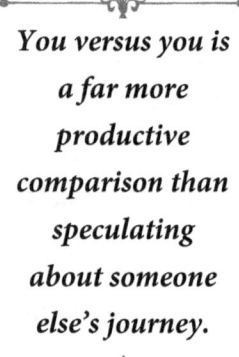

You versus you is a far more productive comparison than speculating about someone else's journey.

How far have you come? What goals have you reached? You versus you is a far more productive comparison than speculating about someone else's journey. Focusing on progressing 1 percent each day is more helpful than comparing your first day to someone's 100th day.

Remain determined and open-minded to discovering how to cultivate and leverage your intrinsic power and gifts. Anyone who told you were anything but capable, wise, resourceful, and powerful was not speaking the truth. You already possess the inner resources you need to transform your life.

Pursuing perfection is a losing game. It is impossible because humanity and flawlessness are incompatible. Regardless of what anyone has told you, including your inner critic, you are worthy of love just as you are right now.

Summary and Self-Care

Recap:

*"When I dare to be powerful, to use my strength in the
service of my vision, then it becomes less and less
important whether I am afraid."*

~ AUDRE LORDE

Break the Cycle

➢ Discover your purpose in this world through trial and
error, courage, and resilience.

➢ Carve out a career path that aligns with your vision,
personality, and values.

➢ Remind yourself of your 100 percent survival rate
whenever you doubt your ability to transform yourself and
revolutionize your ancestral lineage.

➢ Become the adult a younger version of yourself needed
even in the face of backlash.

Live Authentically

➢ Harness courage, self-love, and strength to stand in your
truth.

➢ Remember that no one else in the world has your invaluable
blend of experiences, thoughts, and feelings.

➢ Leverage your authenticity for deep connections and
fulfilling relationships with yourself and others.

➢ Give yourself time, space, and resources to nurture your
authentic self.

Rise to Resilience

➢ Familiarize yourself with the concept of resilience and ways to embody it in your life.

➢ Regularly check in with yourself to assess your emotional temperature.

➢ Consider resources like therapy sessions, somatic movement, and support groups to strengthen your resilience.

➢ Stock your mental health toolbox generously with coping skills to build your fortitude muscle.

Challenge Your Inner Critic

➢ Declare your goals and aspirations to yourself, including the dreams that make you nervous to say out loud.

➢ Confront your inner critic with evidence of your talents and skills that have carried you through adversity—proof that you are far more capable than your inner critic says.

➢ Explore what you need to quiet your inner critic and amplify your inner coach.

➢ Reframe any self-limiting beliefs you are holding onto to cultivate an internal world that is compassionate and loving.

Cycle Breaker Challenge: Practice Radical Self-Care

Break Out of Your Comfort Zone

What if I told you the life you want is in the discomfort you are avoiding? Would you then confront your fears and discomfort if

The life you want is in the discomfort you are avoiding.

you knew your ideal life was at stake? Countless people have a fear of public speaking, however, speaking your mind is essential to cycle-breaking.

Challenge yourself in the next thirty days to speak authentically and publicly about a topic you are passionate about. Your thoughts, experiences, and perspectives are powerful enough to collapse a harmful status quo.

Some ways to push your limits include sharing during a support group, speaking at your local Toastmasters International Club, or speaking your mind on social media.

Build Your Resilience Threshold

Think of a time you tried something challenging for the first time like running the mile or giving a presentation. Did you notice your endurance build through repetition and consistency?

For example, I recently joined a group fitness class. The first few classes I went to pushed me to my limits. I wasn't sure I could continue taking classes. Instead of giving up, however, I continued to challenge myself and modify exercises as needed.

I am now consistently lifting weights and finding exercises to be less daunting. Routinely getting my reps in has increased my stamina and endurance.

What in your life is mentally or physically demanding that you would like to build strength for? Set a target, build a plan, set up an accountability system, and go for it.

Make sure your plan includes ways to release stress. How you release it is totally up to you. You could express confusion through a sketch, channel joy through dancing, or detail fear about a situation in a song.

How you express yourself matters less than the fact that you are safely emptying your emotional bucket to prevent overwhelm.

Move a Muscle, Change a Thought

Choose a physical activity you enjoy to enhance your body-mind connection. Movement can reduce the risk of heart disease, improve sleep, increase mental clarity, and lower anxiety levels.[27] My favorite movement is dancing, because I love the way it makes me feel. I spent afternoons dancing to Selena, El General, and Aaliyah in the living room as a child. I learned that dancing releases "feel good" hormones like serotonin, can reduce cortisol levels, and enhance creativity.

Breaking a sweat is not necessary when it comes to reaping benefits from movement. For instance, volunteering is a distress tolerance skill encouraged under the dialectical behavior therapy framework. Connecting with others is an opportunity to practice mindfulness, enhance interpersonal skills, and reduce negative feelings like loneliness. Pick a cause that aligns with your values and passions, a cardio class that plays your favorite music, or a park to do stretching. What matters is that you move your body and move your life forward.

---

[27] "Benefits of Physical Activity," CDC, April 24, 2024, https://www.cdc.gov/physical-activity-basics/benefits/index.html.

Give Yourself Your Flowers

It is common courtesy to ask others how they are doing, but how common is it for you to extend yourself that courtesy? Your mental health matters as much as anyone else's. One way to nurture your mental wellness is through positive affirmations.

You could practice mirror work by affirming your strengths and worthiness in your reflection. Similarly, you could write positive self-affirmations on sticky notes and place them around your home.

It's okay if you are not comfortable affirming your worthiness. One way to start your mirror work journey is to give thanks to neutral parts of your body that don't upset you.

You might caress your ears and thank them for allowing you to hear your favorite song today or thank your nose for the ability to smell your favorite candle. Gradually, start to affirm other parts of yourself.

Practice Makes Confidence

Actors rehearse their lines before they film a scene. Athletes play scrimmages to prepare for competitions. Musicians do a sound check before a concert. Practicing is key to performing confidently, especially when your quality of life is in jeopardy. Connect with someone you trust such as a friend, therapist, or life coach that you could practice role-playing and setting boundaries.

Another way to practice and prepare for your ideal life is to incorporate visualization. Visualization is a powerful tool to use in goal achievement and on your healing journey.

ONE MORE THING

——————— ꙮ ———————

Your mind is your world. It's your creation. You are the architect, the builder, the artist, the muse, and everything in between. You have the power to actualize the vision you have for your future, the creativity to reframe circumstances to your benefit, and the discernment to curate a support system that nurtures your soul.

No one decides your future for you. People can give their opinions and recommendations. They can share their optimism, pessimism, or indifference. But you decide how you react, pivot, and grow. True freedom is having nothing to prove, explain, or hide from anyone.

Your healing journey is uniquely yours. The specifics of what you need to heal are for you to discover. My hope is that these pages inspire you to take action.

"For every woman who's been told to be quiet, shrink herself, or carry pain that was never hers, this book is your breakthrough. This isn't just a story—it's a movement for those ready to stop the silence, set boundaries, and lead with self-love. Raw, reflective, and radically real, *Break the Cycle Before It Breaks You* is a must-read for cycle breakers everywhere. A masterclass in healing and truth-telling, Priscilla's words are both gut-wrenching and grounding—offering comfort, clarity, and the courage to speak your truth. She doesn't just break the cycle—she lights the way for others to do the same."

~ DR. MORGAN PULLIAM,
Director of Student Involvement at
Illinois Wesleyan University

"Healing doesn't follow a script. It stumbles, repeats, pauses, and rebuilds, and Priscilla María Gutiérrez captures this beautifully. Through personal narrative, cultural insight, and reflection prompts, *Break the Cycle Before It Breaks You* is a gentle guide through the chaos of recovery. This is a story for the ones still in the middle, still unpacking, still unlearning, still getting up. It's not perfect, and that's the point. Healing gets to be human."

~ NICOLE BUCKLEY,
Associate Director of Student Life &
Engagement at Columbia University

You are capable of creating a life you love, no matter what your past looks, sounds, or feels like. I believe in you, and I send you love wherever you are reading this, Cycle Breaker.

ACKNOWLEDGMENTS

T his book is a labor of love, an act of self-love, and a gift to Little Priscilla and Adolescent Priscilla, who daydreamed of becoming an author.

From elementary to law school, my highest grades were in writing-focused classes. Writing has always been a strength of mine. Still, I had to crawl my way to the finish line of this book.

It's one thing to speak your experiences with intangible words that dissolve into the air. It's another to sit down, reflect, and package your deepest pain, joy, and wisdom into adjectives, verbs, and paragraphs. The words on these pages will outlive me. These sentences are memorialized for anyone to read. Owning my truth made this the most challenging writing project I've ever completed.

But I didn't achieve this dream alone. My parents, brother, and fur babies, Nanas and Chules, gave me the love and encouragement I needed to keep feeling, reliving, and writing. Everything I am is rooted in the sacrifices and support of family members. I am the proud product of Latin-American refugees and immigrants who courageously came to the States with dreams. I am forever thankful to those relatives who supported me and my family at pivotal times in our lives. I am especially grateful for the courage of my Abuelita Bertha and Abuelita Gloria to flee to America and provide my parents a better chance at life.

Special thank you to Dr. Michael Ayalon of Greek University and Amanda Varian, my editor, for helping me bring this book to life.

Thank you to all the Brown and Black activists of today and yesterday who have inspired me to speak my mind and take up space. Because of your bravery and sacrifices, I am able to freely express myself in this book and in everyday life.

ABOUT THE AUTHOR

———————— ༄༅༄ ————————

Priscilla María Gutiérrez, J.D., known as the Cycle Breaker Coach on social media, is a certified trauma-informed life coach, keynote speaker, and mental health advocate.

She is also the founder of the Cycle Breakers Club, where she helps members break generational cycles by transforming their mindset, cultivating mindful habits, and setting soul-aligned goals through coaching and community.

She is a sought-after mental health speaker who has led transformative discussions at institutions like Johns Hopkins University, NAMI Florida, and the Alcoholism Center for Women.

She is a proud alumna of Johns Hopkins University and UC Irvine School of Law and shares her healing journey to empower others to live authentically, purposefully, and unapologetically.

When she's not coaching, speaking, or advocating, she finds joy in simple pleasures:

- ➤ **Favorite fruit:** Lemons. Fitting because she's adept at creating lemonade from life's lemons.

- ➤ **Favorite animal:** Dogs. Nature in general strengthens her spirituality.

- ➤ **Favorite colors:** Black and pale pink. In true Priscilla fashion, she embraces duality.

- ➤ **Favorite memory:** Walking around the neighborhood with her Abuelita Bertha and brother Iván X. in Milbrae, California. Not a care in the world. Innocent and happy.

Visit her website at **www.priscillamaria.com** to learn more about her contributions and stay up to date with her impactful work. You can find her on social media as **@CycleBreakerCoach** and email her at **hello@priscillamaria.com**.